Network+™
2005 Q&A

Chimborazo, LLC

THOMSON

COURSE TECHNOLOGY

Professional ■ Trade ■ Reference

ISBN: 1-59200-794-5

Library of Congress Catalog Card Number: 2005921010

Printed in the United States of America

05 06 07 08 09 BH 10 9 8 7 6 5 4 3 2 1

Publisher and GM of Course Technology PTR:
Stacy L. Hiquet

Associate Director of Marketing:
Sarah O'Donnell

Marketing Manager:
Heather Hurley

Manager of Editorial Services:
Heather Talbot

Associate Acquisitions Editor:
Megan Belanger

Senior Editor:
Mark Garvey

Marketing Coordinator:
Jordan Casey

Technical Reviewer:
Marianne Snow

PTR Editorial Services Coordinator:
Elizabeth Furbish

Interior Layout Tech:
William Hartman

Cover Designer:
Mike Tanamachi

Indexer:
FYIndex

Proofreader:
Gene Redding

THOMSON

COURSE TECHNOLOGY
Professional ■ Trade ■ Reference

Thomson Course Technology PTR, a division of Thomson Course Technology
25 Thomson Place ■ Boston, MA 02210 ■ http://www.courseptr.com

CONTENTS

CHAPTER

1

CERTIFICATION

ABOUT THIS CHAPTER

During the last decade, certification has become a very popular way of getting assurance of the skills and capacity of a computer professional. These days, a computer professional can get certification in almost any computer-related area. Network+ is a certification program sponsored by The Computing Technology Industry Association – CompTIA. CompTIA is a non-profit organization with a mission of customer service in the computer industry. In this chapter, you will learn about the Network+ program and determine what requirements you need to meet.

OBJECTIVES

Upon completion of this chapter, you will be able to:

- Describe the Network+ certification program and its purpose.
- Describe the objectives of the certification process.

INTRODUCTION

Credentials are very important in the computer industry. The certification process gives us credentials from an association worthy to render judgment. Once the service technician is certified, both the service technician and the customer will have a higher level of confidence in the work being done.

Network Professional Benefits

- More opportunities for employment without having to go through rigorous testing.
- Professional recognition and career advancement.
- Respect of customers who expect consistent levels of competency.

- Increased value to your organization.

- You can keep ahead of the challenging high-tech environment.

Industry Benefits

- Low costs for employees, since certified people do not need training.

- A more skilled and efficient workforce

- Increased productivity and competitiveness.

- A demonstrated, tangible commitment to your staff and customers.

- Avoidance of the kind of government intervention other industries have had to accept, establishing controls to determine job capability. Service technicians do need a similar type of control to determine excellence, but it is important that the computer industry govern its own technicians and provide its own credentials of competency.

WHAT IS NETWORK+?

The CompTIA Network+ certification is an international industry credential that validates the knowledge of networking professionals with at least nine months of experience in network support or administration or adequate academic training. Earning a Network+ certification demonstrates that the successful candidate knows the layer of the OSI model, can describe the features and functions of a network, and has the skills needed to install, configure, and troubleshoot basic networking hardware peripherals and protocols. A typical candidate should have CompTIA A+ certification or equivalent knowledge, but this is not a prerequisite. Several prestigious technology companies such as Microsoft, Novell, Cisco, Compaq, Lotus, and 3Com recognize CompTIA Network+ as part of their certification track. Many other corporations recommend or require the CompTIA Network+ certification for their IT employees. The skills and knowledge measured by this examination were derived from an industry-wide job task analysis and validated through an industry-wide survey of more than 2,500 participants.

The material covered by this examination can be divided into four domain areas:

- Core Domain 1: Media and Topologies

- Core Domain 2: Protocols and Standards

- Core Domain 3: Network Implementation

- Core Domain 4: Network Support

> **Note** For more information on specific content, please visit the CompTIA Web site at www.comptia.org.

CORE DOMAIN 1: MEDIA AND TOPOLOGIES

Topics covered in this core domain include:

1. Topologies
2. Networking technologies characteristics
3. Cable standards
4. Media types and connectors and their uses
5. Purposes, features, and functions of network components
6. Wireless technologies

CORE DOMAIN 2: PROTOCOLS AND STANDARDS

Topics covered in this domain area include:

1. Identify a MAC (Media Access Control) address and its parts.
2. The OSI Model and its relationship with network components
3. Differences in network protocols
4. IP (Internet Protocol) addresses (IPv4, IPv6) and their classes
5. Identify the purpose of subnetting
6. Identify the differences between private and public network addressing schemes
7. IP (Internet Protocol) addressing methods
8. TCP/IP (Transmission Control Protocol/Internet Protocol) suite protocols
9. Network services and protocols
10. WAN (Wide Area Network) technologies
11. Internet and remote access technologies
12. Security protocols
13. Authentication protocols

CORE DOMAIN 3: NETWORK IMPLEMENTATION

Core domain 3 includes the following objectives:

1. Server operating systems
2. How client workstations connect to and use network resources
3. How to configure a connection in a given scenario
4. Network security aspects (firewall, proxy service, antivirus software, fault tolerance, disaster recovery)
5. VLANs, extranets, and intranets

CORE DOMAIN 4: NETWORK SUPPORT

Core domain 4 includes the following objectives:

1. Troubleshooting techniques
2. Given a network problem scenario, select an appropriate course of action based on a logical troubleshooting strategy

TIPS FOR TAKING THE TEST

Here are some pointers and tips that may help you take these tests:

- Follow a balanced study "diet":
    - Look at an exam topic from several perspectives
    - Understand the actual exam objectives
    - Know your learning preferences and select study methods suited to them
    - Memorizing obvious factual knowledge may not deliver enough
- Practice several times before the actual test
- Get a good night's sleep before the exam day; cramming until the wee hours of the morning will not help you.
- During the test:
    - Slow down and carefully read the questions and all possible answers.
    - Do not read more into the question than what is stated.
    - In multiple-choice questions, eliminate the choices that are not correct and then determine the correct answer from the remaining choices.
    - The BEST choice is always the right choice.
    - Recheck your answers.
    - Remain as calm as possible.

2

DOMAIN 1: MEDIA AND TOPOLOGIES

All questions in this chapter pertain to domain 1, Media and Topologies, of the CompTIA Network+® exam. This domain represents 20% of the total exam and has eight sub-objectives.

For more in-depth information about this domain, see Appendix A, "Network+ (2005) Examination Objectives."

QUESTION 1

The physical layout of a computer network is known as:

- **A.** Protocol
- **B.** Topology
- **C.** Backbone
- **D.** Segment

EXPLANATION

Topology refers to the physical way computer networks are arranged. Common examples are ring, bus, or star formation.

QUESTION 2

The official description for Ethernet can be found on the 802.3 standard from:

- **A.** IETF
- **B.** ACM
- **C.** IEEE
- **D.** CompTIA

EXPLANATION

The most popular form of Ethernet is characterized by the unique way in which devices share a common transmission channel, described in the IEEE 802.3 standard.

QUESTION 3

Token Ring technology is defined in the 802.5 standard from:

A. Xerox
B. CINA
C. AITP
D. IEEE

EXPLANATION

The IEEE has defined Token Ring technology in its 802.5 standard.

QUESTION 4

What is the name of the IEEE project that talks about frame types, addressing, networking connectivity, media, error checking algorithms, and encryption?

A. Project 800
B. Project 80x
C. Project 802
D. Project 802.xx

EXPLANATION

All of these specifications fall under the IEEE's "Project 802," an effort to standardize physical and logical elements of a network.

QUESTION 5

The purpose of this equipment is to convert analog signals into digital signals and vice versa to be transmitted over a computer network.

A. modem
B. phone line
C. repeater
D. hub

EXPLANATION

The word modem reflects its function as a *modulator/demodulator*—that is, it modulates digital signals into analog signals at the transmitting end and then demodulates analog signals into digital signals at the receiving end.

QUESTION 6

What is the name of the technology used to modify analog signals in order to make them suitable for carrying data over a communication path?

    A. Replication

    B. Data modulation

    C. Segmentation

    D. Reassembly

EXPLANATION

In modulation, a simple wave, called a carrier wave, is combined with another analog signal to produce a unique signal that gets transmitted from one node to another.

QUESTION 7

If you are working with a connectivity device that can't accept more than one type of media, you can integrate the two media types by using:

    A. media converters

    B. replication

    C. fiber–optic

    D. UTP cable

EXPLANATION

A media converter is a piece of hardware that enables networks or segments running on different media to interconnect and exchange signals.

QUESTION 8

A media converter is a type of:

    A. hub

    B. UTP cable

    C. fiber–optic

    D. transceiver

EXPLANATION

A transceiver is a device that transmits and receives signals.

QUESTION 9

NICs can be considered a type of:

    A. transceiver
    B. router
    C. bridge
    D. switch

EXPLANATION

A transceiver is a device that transmits and receives signals. Transmitting and receiving signals is an important function of NICs.

QUESTION 10

What type of cable was the foundation for Ethernet networks in the 1970s?

    A. UTP
    B. fiber-optic
    C. coaxial
    D. twisted-pair

EXPLANATION

Coaxial cable remained a popular transmission medium for many years. Over time, however, twisted-pair and fiber-optic cabling have replaced coax in modern LANs. If you work on long-established networks, however, you may have to work with coaxial cable.

QUESTION 11

What type of cable consists of a copper core, metal shielding, and a jacket?

    A. fiber-optic
    B. coaxial
    C. UTP
    D. twisted-pair

EXPLANATION

Coaxial cable consists of a central copper core surrounded by an insulator, braided metal shielding, called *braiding*, and an outer cover called the *sheath* or jacket.

QUESTION 12

With respect to twisted-pair cabling, coaxial cables can carry signals:
- **A.** for more distance
- **B.** for less distance
- **C.** for less time
- **D.** for equal distance

EXPLANATION

It can also carry signals farther than twisted-pair cabling before amplification of the signals becomes necessary.

QUESTION 13

The significant differences between the cable types lie in the materials used for their center cores, which in turn influence their:
- **A.** amplitude
- **B.** frequency
- **C.** range
- **D.** impedance

EXPLANATION

Impedance is the resistance that contributes to controlling the signal, as expressed in ohms.

QUESTION 14

Which of the following has been one of the two Physical layer specifications to transmit data over coaxial cable?
- **A.** ThinPad
- **B.** Thicknet
- **C.** ThingNet
- **D.** Tinynet

EXPLANATION

Historically, data networks have used two Physical layer specifications to transmit data over coaxial cable: thickwire Ethernet and thin Ethernet.

QUESTION 15

The original Ethernet medium, Thicknet, uses:

    A. RG-3

    B. RG-7

    C. RG-8

    D. RG-58A/U

EXPLANATION

RG-8 coaxial cable is approximately 1 cm thick and contains a solid copper core.

QUESTION 16

A popular medium for Ethernet LANs in the 1980s, Thinnet uses:

    A. RG-3

    B. RG-7

    C. RG-8

    D. RG-58A/U

EXPLANATION

RG-58A/U coaxial cable. Its diameter is approximately 0.64 cm, which makes it more flexible and easier to handle and install than Thicknet.

QUESTION 17

When you are connected to the Internet through a broadband cable carrier, which type of coaxial cable does the carrier use?

    A. RG-6

    B. RG-8

    C. RG-58A/U

    D. RG-63T/U

EXPLANATION

The cable that comes into a house from the carrier connects to a cable modem, a device that modulates and demodulates the broadband cable signals using an F-Type connector.

QUESTION 18

This type of cable consists of color-coded pairs of insulated copper wires, each with a diameter of 0.4 to 0.8 mm. Every two wires are twisted around each other to form pairs and all the pairs are encased in a plastic sheath.

A. coaxial
B. twisted-pair
C. fiber-optic
D. coax

EXPLANATION

Twisted-pair is a type of cable similar to telephone wiring that consists of color-coded pairs of insulated copper wires, each with a diameter of 0.4 to 0.8 mm, twisted around each other and encased in plastic coating.

QUESTION 19

Regarding crosstalk problems, what is the effect of having more twists per inch in a pair of wires?

A. The cable is less resistant to crosstalk
B. There is no effect
C. The cable is more resistant to crosstalk
D. The cable is less resistant but thicker

EXPLANATION

Higher-quality, more expensive twisted-pair cable contains more twists per inch.

QUESTION 20

Regarding attenuation problems, what is the effect of having more twists per inch in a pair of wires?

A. A high twist ratio can result in greater attenuation
B. A high twist ratio can result in less attenuation
C. The twist ratio has no effect on the attenuation
D. None of the above

EXPLANATION

Twisting the wire pairs more tightly requires more cable. Attenuation is directly proportional to the signal traveling distance.

QUESTION 21

This type of twisted-pair cable consists of twisted wire pairs that are not only individually insulated, but also surrounded by a shielding made of a metallic substance such as foil:

- **A.** sealed twisted-pair (STP)
- **B.** unprotected twisted-pair (UTP)
- **C.** unshielded twisted-pair (UTP)
- **D.** shielded twisted-pair (STP)

EXPLANATION

All twisted-pair cable falls into one of two categories: shielded twisted-pair (STP) or unshielded twisted-pair (UTP).

QUESTION 22

This type of twisted-pair cable consists of one or more insulated wire pairs encased in a plastic sheath:

- **A.** sealed twisted-pair (STP)
- **B.** unprotected twisted-pair (UTP)
- **C.** unshielded twisted-pair (UTP)
- **D.** shielded twisted-pair (STP)

EXPLANATION

All twisted-pair cable falls into one of two categories: shielded twisted-pair (STP) or unshielded twisted-pair (UTP).

QUESTION 23

Which of the following is true about unshielded twisted-pair (UTP)?

- **A.** UTP is more expensive and more resistant to noise than STP
- **B.** UTP is less expensive and more resistant to noise than STP
- **C.** UTP is more expensive and less resistant to noise than STP
- **D.** None of the above

EXPLANATION

As its name implies, UTP does not contain additional shielding for the twisted pairs. As a result, UTP is both less expensive and less resistant to noise than STP.

2

QUESTION 24

A form of UTP that contains four wire pairs and can carry up to 10 Mbps of data with a possible bandwidth of 16 MHz:

    A. CAT 3
    B. CAT 4
    C. CAT 5
    D. CAT 7

EXPLANATION

CAT 3 has typically been used for 10-Mbps Ethernet or 4-Mbps Token Ring networks.

QUESTION 25

A form of UTP that contains four wire pairs and can support up to 16 Mbps throughput. It is guaranteed for signals as high as 20 MHz and provides more protection against crosstalk and attenuation:

    A. CAT 3
    B. CAT 4
    C. CAT 5
    D. CAT 7

EXPLANATION

CAT 4 may be used for 16 Mbps Token Ring or 10 Mbps Ethernet networks.

QUESTION 26

A form of UTP that contains four wire pairs and supports up to 1000 Mbps throughput and a 100 MHz signal rate:

    A. CAT 4
    B. CAT 5
    C. CAT 6
    D. CAT 7

EXPLANATION

Network administrators are replacing their existing CAT 3 cabling with CAT 5 to accommodate higher throughput.

QUESTION 27

The foil insulation provides excellent resistance to crosstalk and enables this type of cable to support a 250 MHz signaling rate and at least six times the throughput supported by regular CAT 5:

    A. CAT 4

    B. CAT 5

    C. CAT 6

    D. CAT 7

EXPLANATION

CAT 6 is a twisted-pair cable that contains four wire pairs, each wrapped in foil insulation.

QUESTION 28

STP and UTP use this type modular connectors and data jacks:

    A. RJ-4

    B. RJ-10

    C. RJ-23

    D. RJ-45

EXPLANATION

An RJ-45 connector for a cable containing four wire pairs looks similar to analog telephone connectors and jacks, which follow the RJ-11 standard.

QUESTION 29

Popular Ethernet networking standard that replaced the older 10BASE-2 and 10BASE-5 technologies:

    A. 10BASE-T

    B. 10BASE-M

    C. 15BASE-T

    D. 15BASE-M

EXPLANATION

On a 10BASE-T network, one pair of wires is used for transmission, while a second pair of wires is used for reception, allowing 10BASE-T networks to provide full-duplex transmission.

QUESTION 30

A 10BASE-T network requires at least:
- **A.** CAT 1 UTP cabling
- **B.** CAT 3 UTP cabling
- **C.** CAT 5 UTP cabling
- **D.** CAT 7 UTP cabling

EXPLANATION

CAT 3 has typically been used for 10 Mbps Ethernet.

QUESTION 31

What type of topology do nodes on a 10BASE-T Ethernet network use to connect to a central hub or repeater?
- **A.** Token Ring
- **B.** Star
- **C.** Bus
- **D.** Bus ring

EXPLANATION

As is typical of a star topology, a single network cable connects only two devices. Use of the star topology also makes 10BASE-T networks easier to troubleshoot.

QUESTION 32

What is the name of the following rule: Between two communicating nodes, the network cannot contain more than five network segments connected by four repeating devices, and no more than three of the segments may be populated (at least two must be unpopulated)?
- **A.** 3-4-5
- **B.** 4-5-3
- **C.** 4-3-2
- **D.** 5-4-3

EXPLANATION

10BASE-T follows the 5-4-3 rule of networking.

QUESTION 33

What is the maximum distance that a 10BASE-T segment can traverse?

  A. 80 meters
  B. 95 meters
  C. 100 meters
  D. 110 meters

EXPLANATION

To go beyond that distance, Ethernet star segments must be connected by additional hubs or switches to form more complex topologies. This arrangement can connect a maximum of five sequential network segments, for an overall distance between communicating nodes of 500 meters.

QUESTION 34

What is the topology used by nodes on a 100BASE-T network?

  A. Bus
  B. Star
  C. Token Ring
  D. Bus ring

EXPLANATION

100BASE-T uses baseband transmission and the same star topology as 10BASE-T.

QUESTION 35

What is the 100TBASE-T specification you are more likely to find?

  A. 100BASE-TX
  B. 100BASE-TR
  C. 100BASE-TS
  D. 100BASE-TB

EXPLANATION

Two 100BASE-T specifications—100BASE-T4 and 100BASE-TX—have competed for popularity as organizations move to 100-Mbps technology.

QUESTION 36

1000BASE-T achieves its higher throughput by using all four pairs of wires in a:

A. CAT 1 or higher cable
B. CAT 2 or higher cable
C. CAT 3 or higher cable
D. CAT 5 or higher cable

EXPLANATION

Because 1000BASE-T can use existing CAT 5 cabling, the 1-Gigabit technology can be added gradually to an existing 100 Mbps network with minimal interruption of service.

QUESTION 37

What is the maximum distance between communicating nodes on a 1000BASE-T network?

A. 50 meters
B. 100 meters
C. 200 meters
D. 300 meters

EXPLANATION

The maximum segment length on a 1000BASE-T network is 100 meters. It allows for only one repeater.

QUESTION 38

Select all types of fibers that can be used to construct the center or core of a fiber-optic cable: (Choose 2)

A. glass
B. water
C. wood
D. plastic

EXPLANATION

Surrounding the fibers is a layer of glass or plastic called cladding. The cladding is a different density from the glass or plastic in the strands.

QUESTION 39

Select all categories that apply to fiber-optic cable: (Choose 2)

    A. simple-glass
    B. single-mode
    C. multimode
    D. onlymode

EXPLANATION

All fiber cable variations fall into two categories.

QUESTION 40

What is one of the advantages of a single-mode fiber (SMF)?

    A. Reflects light too much
    B. Reflects light very little
    C. Does not reflect light at all
    D. None of the above

EXPLANATION

Because it reflects little, the light does not disperse as the signal travels along the fiber. This continuity allows single-mode fiber to accommodate high bandwidths and long distances.

QUESTION 41

What can be said about multimode fiber (MMF)?

    A. It is more expensive than SMF
    B. It is not reliable
    C. It contains a core with a larger diameter than SMF
    D. None of the above

EXPLANATION

The core on an MMF cable is between 50 and 115 microns in diameter; the most common size is 62.5 microns, while the core on an SMF cable is less than 10 microns in diameter.

QUESTION 42

What is a significant drawback in using fiber?
   A. Its cost
   B. It is not reliable
   C. It is susceptible to noise
   D. Low security levels

EXPLANATION

Fiber–optic cable is the most expensive transmission medium. Because of its cost, most organizations find it impractical to run fiber to every desktop.

QUESTION 43

Which of the following are benefits in using fiber cabling? (Choose 2)
   A. Reliability
   B. Requires special equipment
   C. Throughput
   D. Low security levels

EXPLANATION

Fiber has proved reliable in transmitting data at rates that exceed 10 Gigabits per second. Fiber's amazing throughput is partly due to the physics of light traveling through glass.

QUESTION 44

Which one is a type of connector for fiber cabling?
   A. RJ-45
   B. MT-RJ
   C. RJ-11
   D. RJ-23

EXPLANATION

Here is a list of four connector types: the ST (Straight Tip), SC (Subscriber Connector or Standard Connector), LC (Local Connector), and MT-RJ (Mechanical Transfer Registered Jack).

QUESTION 45

Fiber-optic cabling is resistant to what type of transmission flaw?

    A. Regeneration
    B. Segmentation
    C. Attenuation
    D. EMI

EXPLANATION

Fiber does not conduct electrical current to transmit signals.

QUESTION 46

Depending on the type of fiber-optic cable used, segment lengths vary from 150 to 40,000 meters. This limit is due primarily to:

    A. Cost
    B. Optical loss
    C. Segmentation
    D. EMI

EXPLANATION

Light signal degrades after it travels a certain distance away from its source (just as the light of a flashlight dims after a certain number of feet).

QUESTION 47

What is the name of the IEEE standard for networks using fiber-optic cabling?

    A. 10BASE-T
    B. 10BASE-TX
    C. 10BASE-F
    D. 1000BASE-TX

EXPLANATION

In the 10BASE-F standard, the "10" represents its maximum throughput of 10Mbps, "BASE" indicates its use of baseband transmission, and "F" indicates that it relies on a medium of fiber-optic cable.

QUESTION 48

What is the standard for networks using fiber-optic cabling designed to connect work-stations to a LAN?

    A. 10BASE-FL

    B. 10BASE-FX

    C. 10BASE-LX

    D. None of the above

EXPLANATION

10BASE-FL is designed to connect workstations or to connect two repeaters, while the other two 10BASE-F standards are designed for backbone connections.

QUESTION 49

What is the maximum segment length for 10BASE-FL using repeaters?

    A. 100 meters

    B. 500 meters

    C. 1000 meters

    D. 2000 meters

EXPLANATION

Without repeaters, the maximum segment length for 10BASE-FL is 1000 meters. 10BASE-FL networks may contain no more than two repeaters.

QUESTION 50

What is one the drawbacks of 10BASE-FL?

    A. Security

    B. Cost

    C. Noise resistant

    D. None of the above

EXPLANATION

Because 10BASE-F technologies involve (expensive) fiber and achieve merely 10Mbps throughput (whereas the fiber medium is capable of much higher throughput), it is not commonly found on modern networks.

QUESTION 51

Which transmission modes are supported by 100BASE-FX? (Choose 2)
  A. Broadband
  B. Half-duplex
  C. Full-duplex
  D. Multiband

EXPLANATION

100BASE-FX requires multimode fiber containing at least two strands of fiber. In half-duplex mode, one strand is used for data transmission, while the other strand is used for reception. In full-duplex implementations, both strands are used for both sending and receiving data.

QUESTION 52

100BASE-FX is considered:
  A. Slow Ethernet
  B. Gigabit Ethernet
  C. Millennium Ethernet
  D. Fast Ethernet

EXPLANATION

100BASE-FX, like 100BASE-T, is also described in IEEE's 802.3u standard.

QUESTION 53

Within one network, 100BASE-FX can be easily combined with:
  A. 100BASE-TX
  B. 10BASE-CX
  C. 100BASE-PT
  D. None of the above

EXPLANATION

In order to do this, transceivers in computers and connectivity devices must have both RJ-45 and SC, ST, LC, or MT-RJ ports. Alternatively, a media converter may be used.

QUESTION 54

IEEE specification for a Gigabit Ethernet technology over fiber-optic cabling:
- **A.** 100BASE-TX
- **B.** 100BASE-CX
- **C.** 1000BASE-LX
- **D.** None of the above

EXPLANATION

The "1000" in 1000BASE-LX stands for 1000 Mbps throughput. "BASE" stands for baseband transmission, and "LX" represents its reliance on "long wavelengths."

QUESTION 55

What is the maximum distance that 1000BASE-LX can reach when used with single-mode fiber?
- **A.** 100 meters
- **B.** 550 meters
- **C.** 1000 meters
- **D.** 5000 meters

EXPLANATION

Because of its potential length, 1000BASE-LX is an excellent choice for long back-bones—connecting buildings in a MAN, for example, or connecting an ISP with its telecommunications carrier.

QUESTION 56

With respect to 1000BASE-LX, what can be said about 1000BASE-SX?
- **A.** It is more expensive than 1000BASE-LX
- **B.** It is less expensive than 1000BASE-LX
- **C.** 1000BASE-SX has a bigger throughput
- **D.** 1000BASE-SX also relies on long wavelengths

EXPLANATION

1000BASE-SX relies on only multimode fiber-optic cable as its medium. This makes it "easier" to install than 1000BASE-LX.

QUESTION 57

What does the SX in 1000BASE-SX stand for?

    A. Long wavelengths

    B. Simple transmission

    C. Single strand

    D. Short wavelengths

EXPLANATION

Another difference between 1000BASE-LX and 1000BASE-SX is that 1000BASE-SX uses short wavelengths of 850 nanometers.

QUESTION 58

A measure of the highest frequency of signal a multimode fiber can support over a specific distance measured in MHz-km:

    A. Arrival band

    B. Bandwidth frequency

    C. Modal bandwidth

    D. None of the above

EXPLANATION

It is related to the distortion that occurs when multiple pulses of light, although issued at the same time, arrive at the end of a fiber at slightly different times.

QUESTION 59

What can be said about 1000BASE-SX?

    A. It is best suited for shorter network runs than 1000BASE-LX

    B. It is best suited for larger network runs than 1000BASE-LX

    C. There are no differences between both technologies

    D. None of the above

EXPLANATION

The maximum segment length on a 1000BASE-SX network is between 275 and 550 meters, and only one repeater is accepted.

QUESTION 60

IEEE standard for a 10 Gigabit fiber-optic network:

    A. 10GBASE-TX
    B. 10GBASE-SR
    C. 10GBASE-SX
    D. None of the above

EXPLANATION

"10G" stands for its maximum throughput of 10 Gigabits per second, "BASE" stands for baseband transmission, and "SR" stands for "short-reach."

QUESTION 61

The maximum segment length in a 10GBASE-SR network depends on:

    A. The diameter of the fibers used
    B. The modal bandwidth
    C. The laser power
    D. All of the above

EXPLANATION

For example, if 50-micron fiber is used with the maximum possible modal bandwidth, the maximum segment length is 300 meters. If 62.5-micron fiber is used with the maximum possible modal bandwidth, a 10GBASE-SR segment can be 66 meters long.

QUESTION 62

What is the name of the industry standard for uniform, enterprise-wide, multivendor cabling systems?

    A. Multicabling
    B. Unicabling
    C. Structured cabling
    D. Standard cabling

EXPLANATION

Structured cabling suggests how networking media can best be installed to maximize performance and minimize upkeep.

QUESTION 63

What network topology is assumed by structured cabling?

A. Bus
B. Star
C. Ring
D. All of the above

EXPLANATION

Structured cabling is designed to work just as well for 10BASE-T networks as it does for 1000BASE-LX networks since both networks use the same topology.

QUESTION 64

What is the name of the point at which a building's internal cabling plant begins? (Choose 3)

A. Entrance facility
B. Demarcation point
C. Demarc
D. Telco room

EXPLANATION

The Entrance facility separates LANs from WANs and designates where the telecommunications service carrier accepts responsibility for the (external) wire.

QUESTION 65

What is the name for the wiring system that provides interconnection between telecommunications closets, equipment rooms, and entrance facilities?

A. Central bone
B. Front bone
C. Core wiring
D. Backbone

EXPLANATION

On a campus-wide network, the backbone includes not only vertical connectors between floors, or risers, and cabling between equipment rooms, but also cabling between buildings.

QUESTION 66

What is the name of a "telco room" that contains connectivity for groups of workstations in its area, plus cross connections to equipment rooms?

A. Telecommunication center
B. Telecommunication closets
C. Backbone
D. Horizontal wiring

EXPLANATION

Telecommunication closets typically house patch panels, punch-down blocks, hubs or switches, and possibly other connectivity hardware.

QUESTION 67

What is the maximum allowable distance for horizontal wiring?

A. 20 meters
B. 30 meters
C. 90 meters
D. 100 meters

EXPLANATION

This span includes 90 m to connect a data jack on the wall to the telecommunications closet plus a maximum of 10 m to connect a workstation to the data jack on the wall.

QUESTION 68

What can be said about a patch cable section?

A. It is large
B. It is long
C. It is relatively short
D. None of the above

EXPLANATION

A patch cable is a section of cabling that is usually between 3 and 25 feet long of cabling with connectors on both ends.

QUESTION 69

Select a good practice when cabling a network:
- **A.** Use color-coded cables for different purposes
- **B.** Use the same cable color for everything
- **C.** Do not document your cabling system
- **D.** Keep your cabling system documentation secret even for internal use

EXPLANATION

For example, you might want to use pink for patch cables, green for horizontal wiring, and gray for vertical (backbone) wiring.

QUESTION 70

Select TIA/EIA methods of inserting UTP twisted pairs into RJ-45 plugs: (Choose 2)
- **A.** TIA/EIA 568C
- **B.** TIA/EIA 568A
- **C.** TIA/EIA 558
- **D.** TIA/EIA 568B

EXPLANATION

TIA/EIA has specified two different methods of inserting UTP twisted pairs into an RJ-45 plug. Functionally, there is no difference between the standards.

QUESTION 71

What type of cable is used when two nodes in a network are connected using any connectivity device?
- **A.** Crossover cable
- **B.** Mixed cable
- **C.** Straight-through cable
- **D.** Alt cable

EXPLANATION

A straight-through cable is so named because it allows signals to pass "straight through" between terminations.

QUESTION 72

What type of cable is used when two nodes in a network are connected without using any connectivity device?

A. Crossover cable

B. Mixed cable

C. Straight-through cable

D. Alt cable

EXPLANATION

A crossover cable is a patch cable in which the termination locations of the transmit and receive wires on one end of the cable are reversed.

QUESTION 73

What does WLAN stand for?

A. Wide LAN

B. Wild LAN

C. Web LAN

D. Wireless LAN

EXPLANATION

Networks that transmit signals through the atmosphere are known as wireless networks.

QUESTION 74

What types of signals are typically used by Wireless LANs? (Choose 2)

A. Infrared

B. Radiofrequency (RF)

C. UTP

D. Laser

EXPLANATION

In addition to infrared and RF transmission, microwave and satellite links can be used to transport data through the atmosphere.

QUESTION 75

Regarding wireless networks, a continuum of electromagnetic waves used for data and voice communication is known as:

A. Wireless waves
B. Wireless spectrum
C. Wireless EMI
D. None of the above

EXPLANATION

All wireless signals are carried through the air along electromagnetic waves. On the spectrum, waves are arranged according to their frequencies.

QUESTION 76

In the United States of America, what is the name of the organization that grants other organizations in different locations exclusive rights to use a frequency?

A. FDA
B. OMS
C. FCD
D. FCC

EXPLANATION

The wireless spectrum (as defined by the FCC, which controls its use) spans frequencies between 9 KHz and 300 GHz.

QUESTION 77

Internationally, what is the name of the organization that grants other organizations in different locations exclusive rights to use a frequency?

A. FDA
B. ISO
C. ITU
D. FCC

EXPLANATION

If governments and companies did not adhere to ITU standards, chances are that a wireless device could not be used outside the country in which it was manufactured.

QUESTION 78

The atmosphere is considered a:
- **A.** Guided media
- **B.** Guideless media
- **C.** No media
- **D.** None of the above

EXPLANATION

Because the air provides no fixed path for signals to follow, signals travel without guidance.

QUESTION 79

Where do the wireless signals originate?
- **A.** Electrical current traveling along a conductor
- **B.** The atmosphere
- **C.** The antenna
- **D.** None of the above

EXPLANATION

The electrical signal travels from the transmitter to an antenna, which then emits the signal as a series of electromagnetic waves to the atmosphere.

QUESTION 80

For wireless communication, the antenna is used for: (Choose 2)
- **A.** Transmitting signals
- **B.** Supporting the equipment
- **C.** Decoration
- **D.** Receiving signals

EXPLANATION

As you would expect to exchange information, two antennas must be tuned to the same frequency.

QUESTION 81

What are the factors to consider when choosing an antenna? (Choose 2)

A. Power output
B. Frequency
C. Color-coded cases
D. Antenna color

EXPLANATION

The service's specifications determine the antenna's power output, frequency, and radiation pattern.

QUESTION 82

Type of antenna that issues wireless signals along a single direction:

A. Omni-directional
B. Range
C. Directional
D. Dedicated

EXPLANATION

This type of antenna is used when the source needs to communicate with one destination, as in a point-to-point link.

QUESTION 83

Which type of antenna issues wireless and receives wireless signals with equal strength and clarity in all directions?

A. Omni-directional
B. Range
C. Directional
D. Dedicated

EXPLANATION

This type of antenna is used when many different receivers must be able to pick up the signal, or when the receiver's location is highly mobile.

QUESTION 84

What is the name of the geographical area that an antenna or wireless system can reach?
- **A.** Direction
- **B.** Range
- **C.** Amplitude
- **D.** Frequency

EXPLANATION

Receivers must be within the range to receive accurate signals consistently.

QUESTION 85

Type of antenna propagation where the signal travels directly from its transmitter to its receiver:
- **A.** Omni-directional
- **B.** Reflection
- **C.** Multicast
- **D.** Line-Of-Sight (LOS)

EXPLANATION

Ideally, a wireless signal would travel directly in a straight line from its transmitter to its intended receiver. This type of propagation uses the least amount of energy and results in the reception of the clearest possible signal.

QUESTION 86

What kind of phenomena can happen when an obstacle stands in the signal's way? (Choose 3)
- **A.** Reflection
- **B.** Diffraction
- **C.** Scattering
- **D.** Regeneration

EXPLANATION

The object's geometry governs which of these three phenomena occurs.

QUESTION 87

What is the name for this reaction: The wave encounters an obstacle and bounces back toward its source?

A. Diffraction
B. Reflection
C. Scattering
D. Obstruction

EXPLANATION

A wireless signal will bounce off objects whose dimensions are large compared to the signal's average wavelength.

QUESTION 88

What is the name for this reaction: A wireless signal splits into secondary waves when it encounters an obstruction?

A. Diffraction
B. Reflection
C. Scattering
D. Obstruction

EXPLANATION

Objects with sharp edges—including the corners of walls and desks—cause diffraction.

QUESTION 89

What is the name for diffusion, or reflection in multiple different directions, of a signal?

A. Diffraction
B. Reflection
C. Scattering
D. Obstruction

EXPLANATION

Scattering occurs when a wireless signal encounters an object that has small dimensions compared to the signal's wavelength.

QUESTION 90

What is an advantage of the bouncing nature of wireless signals?
- **A.** Less attenuation
- **B.** They cannot be absorbed by walls
- **C.** They mix with other signals
- **D.** They have a better chance of reaching their destination

EXPLANATION

In environments such as an office building, wireless services depend on signals bouncing off walls, ceilings, floors, and furniture so that they may eventually reach their destination.

QUESTION 91

What is a disadvantage of the multipath nature of wireless signals?
- **A.** Less attenuation
- **B.** They have a better chance of reaching their destination
- **C.** Signal delay
- **D.** They require a more powerful antenna

EXPLANATION

Because of their various paths, multipath signals travel different distances between their transmitter and a receiver. Thus, multiple instances of the same signal can arrive at a receiver at different times.

QUESTION 92

A change in signal strength as a result of some of the electromagnetic energy being scattered, reflected, or diffracted after being issued by the transmitter is known as:
- **A.** Reflection
- **B.** Fading
- **C.** Multipath
- **D.** Extenuation

EXPLANATION

After fading, the strength of the signal that reaches the receiver is lower than the transmitted signal's strength.

QUESTION 93

Which of the following is a problem of wireless signals?

    A. Attenuation

    B. Needs a laser to transmit

    C. Do not need antennas

    D. All of the above

EXPLANATION

As with wire-bound signals, wireless signals also experience attenuation.

QUESTION 94

Select different techniques to fight against attenuation problem with wireless signals: (Choose 2)

    A. Multipath

    B. Amplification

    C. Repetition (Regeneration)

    D. Broadpath

EXPLANATION

Just as with wire-bound transmission, wireless signals are amplified (if analog) or repeated (if digital) to strengthen the signal so that it can be clearly received.

QUESTION 95

What can be said about wireless signals?

    A. Attenuation is the most severe problem

    B. Noise does affect them

    C. Attenuation and interference are the same

    D. Noise does not affect them

EXPLANATION

Interference is a significant problem for wireless communications because the atmosphere is saturated with electromagnetic waves.

QUESTION 96

Wireless LANs may be affected by: (Choose 3)
- **A.** cellular phones
- **B.** mobile phones
- **C.** overhead lights
- **D.** basement lights

EXPLANATION

Interference is a significant problem for wireless communications because the atmosphere is saturated with electromagnetic waves.

QUESTION 97

What can be said about wireless signals with respect to wire-bound signals?
- **A.** Both are equally vulnerable to EMI
- **B.** Wire-bound signals are more vulnerable to noise
- **C.** Wire-bound signals are less protected
- **D.** Wireless signals are more vulnerable to noise

EXPLANATION

Wireless signals cannot depend on a conduit or shielding to protect them from extraneous EMI.

QUESTION 98

Transmission technology where the transmitter concentrates the signal energy at a single frequency or in a very small range of frequencies:
- **A.** Broadband
- **B.** Narrowband
- **C.** Multiband
- **D.** Spread spectrum

EXPLANATION

In contrast to narrowband, broadband uses a relatively wide band of the wireless spectrum.

QUESTION 99

Transmission technology where the transmitter uses a wide range of frequencies:

    A. Broadband
    B. Narrowband
    C. Uniband
    D. Spread spectrum

EXPLANATION

Broadband technologies, as a result of their wider frequency bands, offer higher throughputs than narrowband technologies.

QUESTION 100

Transmission technology where the transmitter uses multiple frequencies to transmit a signal:

    A. Broadband
    B. Narrowband
    C. Multiband
    D. Spread spectrum

EXPLANATION

Spread spectrum technology takes its name from the fact that the signal is spread out over the wireless spectrum.

QUESTION 101

What can be said about spread spectrum regarding narrowband technologies?

    A. Spread spectrum requires more power per frequency
    B. Spread spectrum signals are more likely to interfere with narrowband signals traveling in the same frequency band
    C. Spread spectrum requires less power per frequency
    D. Spread spectrum requires equal power per frequency

EXPLANATION

In contrast to narrowband, broadband uses a relatively wide band of the wireless spectrum.

QUESTION 102

This is one specific implementation of spread spectrum:

A. DNSS
B. FHSS
C. EMIS
D. FHNS

EXPLANATION

In FHSS transmission, a signal jumps between several different frequencies within a band in a synchronization pattern known only to the channel's receiver and transmitter.

QUESTION 103

This is one specific implementation of spread spectrum:

A. DNSS
B. FNSS
C. EMIS
D. DSSS

EXPLANATION

In DSSS, a signal's bits are distributed over an entire frequency band at once. Each bit is coded so that the receiver can reassemble the original signal upon receiving the bits.

QUESTION 104

What can be said about fixed wireless systems?

A. Both transmitter and receiver do not move
B. Transmitter can move
C. Receiver can move
D. Transmitter can move but receiver cannot move

EXPLANATION

One advantage of fixed wireless is that because the receiver's location is predictable, energy need not be wasted issuing signals across a large geographical area.

QUESTION 105

What can be said about mobile wireless systems?

    A. Both transmitter and receiver do not move

    B. Receiver can move only outside transmitter's range

    C. Receiver can move within transmitter's range

    D. Transmitter can move but receiver cannot move

EXPLANATION

This allows the receiver to roam from one place to another while continuing to pick up its signal.

QUESTION 106

What can be said about infrared signals?

    A. They are transmitted at frequencies within the wireless spectrum

    B. They are transmitted at frequencies below the wireless spectrum

    C. They are transmitted at the same set of frequencies as wireless

    D. They are transmitted at frequencies above the wireless spectrum

EXPLANATION

Infrared signals are transmitted at frequencies in the 300 GHz to 300,000 GHz range.

QUESTION 107

What can be said about infrared frequencies?

    A. They cannot be used to transmit data through space

    B. They approach the range of visible light

    C. They all are within the range of visible light

    D. They can only be seen at night

EXPLANATION

Some infrared frequencies can be seen.

QUESTION 108

What is one advantage of infrared signals over wireless signals?
  A. Infrared requires less power
  B. Infrared travels farther
  C. Infrared maneuvers around obstacles less successfully
  D. High throughput

EXPLANATION

Infrared technology has the potential to transmit data at speeds that rival fiber-optic.

QUESTION 109

What is one disadvantage of infrared signals over wireless signals?
  A. Wireless requires more power
  B. Wireless travels less distance
  C. Infrared maneuvers around obstacles less successfully
  D. Infrared cannot be used to connect two computers in the same room

EXPLANATION

Infrared exchange relies on the devices being close to each other and in some cases, with a clear, line-of-sight path between them.

QUESTION 110

The most common form of WLAN relies on:
  A. Lower frequencies
  B. Higher frequencies
  C. Middle range frequencies
  D. FCC licensed frequencies

EXPLANATION

The most common form of WLAN relies on frequencies in the 2.4-2.4835 GHz band (more commonly known as the "2.4 GHz band") to send and receive signals.

QUESTION 111

The most common form of WLAN relies on:

    A. Higher frequencies
    B. Middle range frequencies
    C. FCC licensed frequencies
    D. FCC unlicensed frequencies

EXPLANATION

The most common form of WLAN relies on frequencies in the 2.4-2.4835 GHz band (more commonly known as the "2.4 GHz band") to send and receive signals.

QUESTION 112

What can be said about an ad hoc WLAN?

    A. It works well for large wireless networks
    B. It requires connectivity devices to work
    C. It doesn't requires connectivity devices to work
    D. It works well for a network with many users

EXPLANATION

In an ad hoc WLAN, wireless nodes, or stations, transmit directly to each other via wireless NICs.

QUESTION 113

Device that accepts wireless signals from multiple nodes and retransmits them to the rest of the network:

    A. Antenna
    B. Access point
    C. Transceiver
    D. Spectrumer

EXPLANATION

Instead of communicating directly with each other in ad hoc mode, stations on WLANs can use the infrastructure mode, which depends on an intervening connectivity device called an access point.

QUESTION 114

Besides sufficient power, what else is needed by an access point to cover its intended range?

    A. Be completely shielded
    B. Be placed behind glass walls
    C. Be placed on a dark room
    D. Be strategically placed

EXPLANATION

If an access point must serve a group of workstations in several offices on one floor in a building, it should probably be located in an open area near the center of that floor.

QUESTION 115

How many access points can be used on a wireless network using infrastructure mode?

    A. None
    B. Exactly 1
    C. No more than 2
    D. Several

EXPLANATION

The number of access points depends on the number of stations a WLAN connects.

QUESTION 116

What is the maximum number of stations an access point can serve?

    A. From 3 to 5
    B. Exactly 5
    C. From 10 to 100
    D. Unlimited

EXPLANATION

The maximum number of stations each access point can serve varies, depending on the wireless technology used.

QUESTION 117

What is the maximum recommended distance for a station to be separated from its access point?

- **A.** 5 meters
- **B.** 150 meters
- **C.** More than 150 meters
- **D.** Less than 300 feet

EXPLANATION

In general, stations must remain within 300 feet of an access point to maintain optimal transmission speeds.

QUESTION 118

What can be said about wireless technology?

- **A.** It can be used to connect different parts of a LAN
- **B.** It cannot be used to connect two separate LANs
- **C.** It connects only multiple nodes within a LAN
- **D.** None of the above

EXPLANATION

In addition to connecting multiple nodes within a LAN, wireless technology can use a fixed link with directional antennas to connect two access points.

QUESTION 119

When connecting two WLANs, what is the maximum distance between access points?

- **A.** Less than 300 feet
- **B.** Less than 1000 feet
- **C.** More than 1000 meters
- **D.** As far as 1500 meters

EXPLANATION

In the case of connecting two WLANs, access points could be as far as 1000 feet apart.

QUESTION 120

What can be said about WLANs regarding wire-bound networks?
- **A.** They have to use different network protocols
- **B.** They have to use different operating systems
- **C.** They both use the same protocols and operating systems
- **D.** They are not compatible

EXPLANATION

WLANs and wire-bound networks are compatible. This compatibility ensures that wireless and wire-bound transmission methods can be integrated on the same network.

QUESTION 121

What can be said about WLANs regarding wire-bound networks?
- **A.** They both use the same signaling techniques
- **B.** They use the same signaling techniques but different operating systems
- **C.** They use different signaling techniques and network protocols
- **D.** They use different signaling techniques

EXPLANATION

Only the signaling techniques differ between wireless and wire-bound portions of a LAN.

QUESTION 122

What can be said about WLAN standards?
- **A.** They all have the same techniques for generating and encoding wireless signals
- **B.** They have different techniques for generating and encoding wireless signals
- **C.** They use different network protocols than wire-bound networks
- **D.** All of the above

EXPLANATION

Techniques vary from one WLAN standard to another.

QUESTION 123

The device inside a computer that connects a computer to the network media, thus allowing it to communicate with other computers:

A. Motherboard
B. Fax
C. Hard disk
D. NIC

EXPLANATION

NICs are also known as network adapters.

QUESTION 124

If a NIC works on a workstation, what can be assumed about that NIC?

A. It might not work on all workstations
B. It will work on all workstations
C. A NIC will always work
D. All of the above

EXPLANATION

Different PCs and network types require different kinds of network interface cards.

QUESTION 125

The physical or atmospheric means through which data is transmitted and received:

A. Router
B. Transmission media
C. Protocol
D. All of the above

EXPLANATION

Transmission media may be physical, such as wire or cable, or atmospheric (wireless), such as radio waves.

2

QUESTION 126

How many fundamental types of physical topologies can be defined?

   A. 2
   B. 3
   C. 5
   D. 6

EXPLANATION

Physical topologies are divided into these fundamental geometric shapes: bus, ring, and star.

QUESTION 127

What is the topology that consists of a single cable connecting all nodes on a network without intervening connectivity devices?

   A. Ring
   B. Star
   C. Ring-Star
   D. Bus

EXPLANATION

The single cable is called the bus and can support only one channel for communication; as a result, every node shares the bus's total capacity.

QUESTION 128

On what network topology are the devices responsible for getting data from one point to another?

   A. Star
   B. Star-Ring
   C. Bus
   D. Ring

EXPLANATION

Each node on a bus network passively listens for data directed to it. When one node wants to transmit, it broadcasts an alert to the entire network, informing all nodes that a transmission is being sent; the destination node then picks up the transmission.

QUESTION 129

What is the purpose of a terminator?

    A. Stop signals after they have reached the end of the wire

    B. Specify the destination node

    C. Specify the source node

    D. Prevent other nodes from listening to a message

EXPLANATION

Without terminators, signals on a bus network would travel endlessly between the two ends of the network.

QUESTION 130

What can happen as a result of a signal bounce?

    A. Only the intended recipient gets a message

    B. Every node knows who is the sender of a message

    C. Every node knows who is the recipient of a message

    D. New messages could not be sent

EXPLANATION

Signal bounce will not allow new signals to get through the media.

QUESTION 131

What is the physical topology where each node is connected to the two nearest nodes so that the entire network forms a circle?

    A. Bus

    B. Ring

    C. Star

    D. Bus-Star

EXPLANATION

In a ring topology, data is transmitted clockwise, in one direction (unidirectionally) around the ring.

2

QUESTION 132

What is true about a ring topology?
- **A.** Like a bus topology, data does not stop at its destination
- **B.** Like a bus topology, it also needs terminators
- **C.** It is an active topology
- **D.** It is bidirectional

EXPLANATION

In a ring topology, each workstation acts as a repeater for the transmission.

QUESTION 133

What are some of the disadvantages of a ring topology? (Choose 2)
- **A.** It does not scale well
- **B.** A single malfunctioning workstation can disable the entire network
- **C.** It is very flexible
- **D.** It is a bidirectional topology

EXPLANATION

If one workstation has a malfunctioning NIC, your message will never reach its destination. In addition, the response time is directly proportional to the number of nodes on the network.

QUESTION 134

What is the physical topology where every node on the network is connected through a central device, such as a hub or switch?
- **A.** Bus
- **B.** Ring
- **C.** Star
- **D.** Bus-Ring

EXPLANATION

Any single cable on a star network connects only two devices (for example, a workstation and a hub).

QUESTION 135

What are some of the advantages of a star network? (Choose 2)
- **A.** Fault-tolerant
- **B.** Requires less cable than bus
- **C.** Requires less cable than ring
- **D.** It can easily be moved, isolated, or interconnected with other networks

EXPLANATION

A single malfunctioning workstation cannot disable an entire star network. Single star networks are commonly interconnected with other networks through hubs and switches to form more complex topologies.

QUESTION 136

What are some of the disadvantages of a star network? (Choose 2)
- **A.** Less secure
- **B.** Requires more cable than bus
- **C.** Requires more cable than ring
- **D.** Less scalable than bus or ring

EXPLANATION

Star topologies require more cabling than ring or bus networks. They also require more configuration work.

QUESTION 137

What is the purpose of a network's access method?
- **A.** Control traffic
- **B.** Avoid collisions
- **C.** Make the bandwidth unlimited for the network
- **D.** Limit the network bandwidth

EXPLANATION

A network's access method is its method of controlling how network nodes access the communications channel.

2

QUESTION 138

What does CSMA/CD stand for?
- **A.** Carrier Service Multiple Access with Collision Detection
- **B.** Carrier Sense Multiple Access with Collision Avoidance
- **C.** Carrier Sense Multiple Access with Collision Detection
- **D.** Control Sense Multiple Access with Collision Direction

EXPLANATION

The access method used in Ethernet is called Carrier Sense Multiple Access with Collision Detection (CSMA/CD).

QUESTION 139

What will a NIC on an Ethernet do in case of a collision?
- **A.** It will immediately stop transmitting
- **B.** It will keep transmitting
- **C.** It will wait for 10 minutes before transmitting again
- **D.** It will wait for 2 minutes before transmitting again

EXPLANATION

In the event of a collision, the network performs a series of steps known as the collision detection routine.

QUESTION 140

What can be said about collisions?
- **A.** A collision rate greater than 5% of all traffic is pretty common
- **B.** Collisions does not occur on Ethernet
- **C.** Collisions cannot corrupt data on transit
- **D.** On heavily trafficked networks, collisions are fairly common

EXPLANATION

It is not surprising that the more nodes there are transmitting data on a network, the more collisions that will take place.

QUESTION 141

What connectivity device enables multiple nodes to simultaneously transmit and receive data over different logical network segments?

A. Hub
B. Repeater
C. Switch
D. Amplifier

EXPLANATION

A switch can separate a network segment into smaller segments, with each segment being independent of the others and supporting its own traffic.

QUESTION 142

How many types of Ethernet frames can be found on a network?

A. 3
B. 4
C. 6
D. 7

EXPLANATION

Ethernet networks may use one (or a combination) of four kinds of data frames: Ethernet_802.2 ("Raw"), Ethernet_802.3 ("Novell proprietary"), Ethernet_II ("DIX"), and Ethernet_SNAP.

QUESTION 143

What can be expected from Ethernet frames?

A. You cannot use multiple frame types on a network
B. Ethernet frames can only carry TCP/IP packets
C. Ethernet frames are related to higher-level layers of the OSI Model
D. Ethernet frame types have no relation to the topology or cabling characteristics of the network

EXPLANATION

Physical layer standards, such as 10BASE-T or 100BASE-TX, have no effect on the type of framing that occurs in the Data Link layer.

2

QUESTION 144

NICs can automatically sense what types of frames are running on a network and adjust themselves to that specification. What is the name of this feature?

    A. Auto-detect

    B. Auto-configuration

    C. Auto-framing

    D. Auto-diagnosis

EXPLANATION

Workstations, networked printers, and servers added to an existing network can all take advantage of auto-detection.

QUESTION 145

What Ethernet frame was developed by DEC, Intel, and Xerox before the IEEE began to standardize Ethernet?

    A. Ethernet_II ("DIX")

    B. Ethernet_802.2

    C. Ethernet_802.3

    D. Ethernet_SNAP

EXPLANATION

DEC, Intel, and Xerox can be abbreviated as "DIX."

QUESTION 146

What does HSTR stand for?

    A. High Speed Transfer Rate

    B. High Speed Transmission Rate

    C. High Speed Token Ring

    D. High Speed Transmission Recovery

EXPLANATION

HSTR can use either twisted-pair or fiber-optic cable as its transmission medium, and it is the fastest Token Ring standard capable of transmitting at 100 Mbps.

QUESTION 147

What type of physical topology does a Token Ring network use?

    A. Bus

    B. Star-Ring

    C. Star

    D. Ring

EXPLANATION

Token Ring networks use the token-passing routine and a star-ring hybrid physical topology.

QUESTION 148

What can be said about Token Ring when compared to Ethernet? (Choose 2)

    A. Token Ring is more reliable and efficient than Ethernet

    B. Collisions do not occur on Token Ring

    C. Like Ethernet, Token Ring also uses CSMA/CD

    D. Like Ethernet, Token Ring also uses CSMA/CA

EXPLANATION

The token passing control scheme avoids the possibility for collisions. It also does not impose distance limitations on the length of a LAN segment, unlike CSMA/CD.

QUESTION 149

What type of signaling do IEEE 802.11 techniques use?

    A. Half-Duplex

    B. Duplex

    C. Full-Duplex

    D. Simplex

EXPLANATION

Wireless station using one of the 802.11 techniques can either transmit or receive but cannot do both simultaneously (assuming the station has only one transceiver installed, as is usually the case).

2

QUESTION 150

What type of access method do IEEE 802.11 standards use?

A. CSMA/CD
B. Token passing
C. CSMA/AD
D. CSMA/CA

EXPLANATION

802.11 standards specify the use of Carrier Sense Multiple Access with Collision Avoidance to access a shared medium.

QUESTION 151

Which of the following statements about CSMA/CA is true?

A. CSMA/CA eliminates collisions
B. CSMA/CA is faster than CSMA/CD
C. Collisions are less likely to occur with CSMA/CA
D. CSMA/CA has less overhead than CSMA/CD

EXPLANATION

Compared to CSMA/CD, CSMA/CA minimizes, but does not eliminate, the potential for collisions.

QUESTION 152

What protocol can be used to reserve the medium for one station's use?

A. CSMA/CD
B. RTS/CTS
C. RTD/CTD
D. CSMA/CA

EXPLANATION

RTS/CTS enables a source node to issue an RTS signal to an access point requesting the exclusive opportunity to transmit.

QUESTION 153

What IEEE 802.11 standard signals are less likely to suffer interference from microwave ovens and cordless phones?

   A. 802.11a
   B. 802.11b
   C. 802.11c
   D. 802.11g

EXPLANATION

The 802.11a standard uses multiple frequency bands in the 5 GHz frequency range that is not as congested as the 2.4 GHz band.

QUESTION 154

What IEEE 802.11 standards are compatible?

   A. 802.11a and 802.11b
   B. 802.11b and 802.11.c
   C. 802.11g and 802.11c
   D. None of the above

EXPLANATION

802.11g, like 802.11b, uses the 2.4 GHz frequency band.

QUESTION 155

What type of signaling does Bluetooth use?

   A. DSSS
   B. FDM
   C. FDDI
   D. FHSS

EXPLANATION

Bluetooth is a mobile wireless networking standard that uses FHSS (frequency hopping spread spectrum) RF signaling in the 2.4-GHz band.

QUESTION 156

How far can communicating nodes be when using Bluetooth version 2.0?

A. 30 meters
B. 50 meters
C. 75 meters
D. 100 meters

EXPLANATION

When using Bluetooth version 2.0, communicating nodes can be as far as approximately 100 feet apart.

QUESTION 157

What type does PAN stand for?

A. Point Access Name
B. Personal Area Network
C. Point Access Network
D. Personal Application Network

EXPLANATION

Bluetooth was designed to be used on PANs or small networks of personal communication devices.

QUESTION 158

How many slaves units can a piconet have when using Bluetooth 2.0?

A. 4
B. 5
C. 7
D. More than 7

EXPLANATION

With Bluetooth 2.0, the number of slaves on a piconet is unlimited.

QUESTION 159

What is true about infrared signals?
  A. IR signals cannot operate on a multipath fashion
  B. IR signals can pass through a wall
  C. IR signals must follow an unobstructed path between sender and receiver
  D. Communicating computers using IR signals must be at least 3 meters apart

EXPLANATION

In general, infrared signals depend on a line-of-sight transmission path between the sender and receiver.

QUESTION 160

What is a benefit of using infrared signals?
  A. Cost
  B. Reliability
  C. Security
  D. Can circumnavigate obstacles easily

EXPLANATION

Like Bluetooth, IR technology is relatively inexpensive.

ANSWER GRID FOR DOMAIN 1

Question	Answer	Objective	Question	Answer	Objective
1	B	1.1	16	D	1.5
2	C	1.2	17	A	1.4
3	D	1.2	18	B	1.5
4	C	1.2	19	C	1.5
5	A	1.6	20	A	1.5
6	B	1.6	21	D	1.5
7	A	1.6	22	C	1.5
8	D	1.6	23	D	1.5
9	A	1.6	24	A	1.5
10	C	1.5	25	B	1.5
11	B	1.5	26	B	1.5
12	A	1.5	27	C	1.5
13	D	1.5	28	D	1.4
14	B	1.5	29	A	1.2, 1.3
15	C	1.5	30	B	1.2, 1.3

Question	Answer	Objective
31	B	1.2, 1.3
32	D	1.2, 1.3
33	C	1.2, 1.3
34	B	1.2, 1.3
35	A	1.2, 1.3
36	D	1.2, 1.3
37	C	1.2, 1.3
38	A, D	1.5
39	B, C	1.5
40	B	1.5
41	C	1.5
42	A	1.5
43	A, C	1.5
44	B	1.4
45	D	1.5
46	B	1.5
47	C	1.2, 1.3
48	A	1.2, 1.3
49	D	1.2, 1.3
50	B	1.2, 1.3
51	B, C	1.2, 1.3
52	D	1.2, 1.3
53	A	1.2, 1.3
54	C	1.2, 1.3
55	D	1.2, 1.3
56	B	1.2, 1.3
57	D	1.2, 1.3
58	C	1.2, 1.3
59	A	1.2, 1.3
60	B	1.2, 1.3
61	A	1.2, 1.3
62	C	1.2
63	B	1.2
64	A, B, C	1.2
65	D	1.2
66	B	1.2
67	D	1.2
68	C	1.2
69	A	1.2
70	B, D	1.2

Question	Answer	Objective
71	C	1.4
72	A	1.4
73	D	1.7
74	A, B	1.7
75	B	1.7
76	D	1.7
77	C	1.7
78	B	1.7
79	A	1.7
80	A, D	1.7
81	A, B	1.7
82	C	1.7
83	A	1.7
84	B	1.7
85	D	1.7
86	A, B, C	1.7
87	B	1.7
88	A	1.7
89	C	1.7
90	D	1.7
91	C	1.7
92	B	1.7
93	A	1.7
94	B, C	1.7
95	B	1.7
96	A, B, C	1.7
97	D	1.7
98	B	1.7
99	A	1.7
100	D	1.7
101	C	1.7
102	B	1.7
103	D	1.7
104	A	1.7
105	C	1.7
106	D	1.7
107	B	1.7
108	D	1.7
109	C	1.7
110	A	1.7

Question	Answer	Objective
111	D	1.7
112	C	1.7
113	B	1.7
114	D	1.7
115	D	1.7
116	C	1.7
117	D	1.7
118	A	1.7
119	B	1.7
120	C	1.7
121	D	1.7
122	B	1.7
123	D	1.6
124	A	1.6
125	B	1.5
126	B	1.1
127	D	1.1
128	C	1.1
129	A	1.1
130	D	1.1
131	B	1.1
132	C	1.1
133	A, B	1.1
134	C	1.1
135	A, D	1.1

Question	Answer	Objective
136	B, C	1.1
137	B	1.2
138	C	1.2
139	A	1.2
140	D	1.2
141	C	1.2
142	B	1.2
143	D	1.2
144	A	1.2
145	A	1.2
146	C	1.2
147	B	1.2
148	A, B	1.2
149	A	1.7
150	D	1.7
151	C	1.7
152	B	1.7
153	A	1.7
154	C	1.7
155	D	1.7
156	A	1.7
157	B	1.7
158	D	1.7
159	C	1.7
160	A	1.7

3

DOMAIN 2: PROTOCOLS AND STANDARDS

All questions in this chapter pertain to domain 2, Protocols and Standards, of the CompTIA Network+® exam. This domain represents 20% of the total exam and has 18 sub-objectives.

For more in-depth information about this domain, see Appendix A, "Network+ (2005) Examination Objectives."

QUESTION 1

How many layers does the OSI Model have for network communications?

    A. 10

    B. 5

    C. 7

    D. 4

EXPLANATION

The OSI Model divides network communications into Physical, Data Link, Network, Transport, Session, Presentation, and Application layers.

QUESTION 2

To communicate with another node, a device initiates a data exchange through what OSI Model layer?

    A. Transport

    B. Physical

    C. Network

    D. Application

EXPLANATION

The Application layer separates data into *protocol data units (PDUs)*. From there, PDUs progress down through OSI Model layers 6, 5, 4, 3, 2, and 1 before being issued to the network medium.

QUESTION 3

For the OSI Model, logically, each layer communicates from one computer to another with:

A. the same layer
B. the layer below
C. the layer above
D. any higher layer

EXPLANATION

For the OSI Model, logically the Application layer protocols on one computer exchange information with the Application layer protocols of the second computer.

QUESTION 4

What layer of the OSI Model facilitates communication between software applications and lower-layer network services?

A. Data Link
B. Application
C. Session
D. Transport

EXPLANATION

Through Application layer protocols, software programs negotiate their formatting, procedural, security, synchronization, and other requirements with the network.

QUESTION 5

What layer of the OSI Model serves as a translator for system applications?

A. Transport
B. Session
C. Presentation
D. Network

EXPLANATION

Protocols at the Presentation layer accept Application layer data and format it so that one type of application and host can understand data from another type of application and host.

QUESTION 6

What layer of the OSI Model manages data encryption and decryption?
  A. Presentation
  B. Session
  C. Data Link
  D. Physical

EXPLANATION

When you look up your bank account over a secure connection, Presentation layer protocols will encrypt your account data before it is transmitted. On your end of the network, the Presentation layer will decrypt the data as it is received.

QUESTION 7

Which of the following terms refers to a connection for ongoing data exchange between two parties?
  A. link
  B. session
  C. traffic
  D. medium

EXPLANATION

Today, the term *session* is often used in the context of a connection between a remote client and an access server or between a Web browser client and a Web server.

QUESTION 8

Protocols on this layer coordinate and maintain communications between two nodes on the network:
  A. Application
  B. Presentation
  C. Data Link
  D. Session

EXPLANATION

Among the Session layer's functions are establishing and keeping alive the communications link for the duration of the session, keeping the communication secure, and synchronizing the dialog between the two nodes.

QUESTION 9

What layer of the OSI Model is responsible for accepting data from the Session layer and managing end-to-end delivery of data?

    A. Data Link
    B. Session
    C. Transport
    D. Network

EXPLANATION

Protocols in the Transport layer can ensure that the data is transferred from point A to point B reliably, in the correct sequence, and without errors.

QUESTION 10

Transport layer protocols that establish a connection with another node before they begin transmitting data are known as:

    A. connectionless protocols
    B. syn-oriented protocols
    C. connection-oriented protocols
    D. ack-oriented protocols

EXPLANATION

TCP is one example of a connection-oriented protocol. In the case of requesting a Web page, only after TCP establishes a connection does it transmit the HTTP request for a Web page.

QUESTION 11

To ensure data integrity further, connection-oriented protocols such as TCP use a:

    A. digital signature
    B. digital certificate
    C. symmetric encryption algorithm
    D. checksum

EXPLANATION

A checksum is a unique character string that allows the receiving node to determine if an arriving data unit matches exactly the data unit sent by the source.

QUESTION 12

What kind of Transport layer protocols are more useful in situations where data must be transferred quickly?

    A. connectionless protocols

    B. syn-oriented protocols

    C. connection-oriented protocols

    D. ack-oriented protocols

EXPLANATION

A connectionless protocol's lack of sophistication makes it more efficient than a connection-oriented protocol.

QUESTION 13

What layer of the OSI Model is in charge of translating network addresses into their physical counterparts and decides how to route data from the sender to the receiver?

    A. Transport

    B. Network

    C. Session

    D. Physical

EXPLANATION

Network layer protocols accept the Transport layer segments and add logical addressing information in a network header. Network layer protocols also determine the path from point A on one network to point B on another network.

QUESTION 14

What is the name of the process of determining the best communication path over a computer network?

    A. Routing

    B. Communicating

    C. Linking

    D. Connecting

EXPLANATION

Route means to direct data intelligently based on addressing, patterns of usage, and availability.

QUESTION 15

Regarding the OSI Model, routers belong to the:

    A. Physical layer

    B. Data Link layer

    C. Session layer

    D. Network layer

EXPLANATION

Routers are the devices that connect network segments and direct data.

QUESTION 16

The process when a Network layer protocol subdivides the segments it receives from the Transport layer into smaller packets is known as:

    A. segmentation

    B. sequencing

    C. fragmentation

    D. reassembly

EXPLANATION

Fragmentation accomplishes the same task at the Network layer that segmentation performs in the Transport layer. It makes certain that packets issued to the network are no larger than the network's maximum transmission unit size.

QUESTION 17

In what layer of the OSI Model is the data received from the Network layer divided into distinct frames that can then be transmitted by the Physical layer?

    A. Transport

    B. Network

    C. Session

    D. Data Link

EXPLANATION

Suppose you are in Ms. Jones's large classroom. You might say, "Ms. Jones? Can you explain more about the effects of railroads on commerce in the mid-nineteenth century?" You have formatted your thought as a question, just as the Data Link layer formats data into frames that can be interpreted by receiving computers.

QUESTION 18

In the Data Link layer for the OSI Model, error checking is accomplished by a:

A. 3-byte Frame Check Sequence (FCS)
B. 4-byte Frame Check Sequence (FCS)
C. 5-byte Frame Check Sequence (FCS)
D. 6-byte Frame Check Sequence (FCS)

EXPLANATION

The purpose of a 4-byte Frame Check Sequence (FCS) is to ensure that the data at the destination exactly matches the data issued from the source.

QUESTION 19

What sublayer of the Data Link layer for the OSI Model manages access to the physical medium?

A. Media Access Control (MAC)
B. Logical Link Control (LLC)
C. Medium Access Control (MAC)
D. Memory Access Control (MAC)

EXPLANATION

The Media Access Control (MAC) appends the physical address of the destination computer onto the data frame. Because this address is appended by the MAC sublayer of the Data Link layer, it also known as a MAC address.

QUESTION 20

How many parts does the MAC address contain?

A. 1
B. 2
C. 3
D. 4

EXPLANATION

The combination of the Block ID and Device ID result in a unique, 12-character MAC address.

QUESTION 21

What is the size of a full MAC address?

- **A.** 10 characters
- **B.** 11 characters
- **C.** 12 characters
- **D.** 15 characters

EXPLANATION

The combination of the Block ID and Device ID results in a unique, 12-character MAC address.

QUESTION 22

Protocols at the Physical layer accept frames from the Data Link layer and transmit signals generating:

- **A.** voltage
- **B.** packets
- **C.** bytes
- **D.** frames

EXPLANATION

When receiving data, Physical layer protocols detect voltage and accept signals, which they pass on to the Data Link layer.

QUESTION 23

Besides the Data Link layer, NICs also operate at the:

- **A.** Session layer
- **B.** Physical layer
- **C.** Network layer
- **D.** Transport layer

EXPLANATION

When you install a NIC in your desktop PC and connect it to a cable, you are establishing the foundation that allows the computer to be networked. In other words, you are providing a Physical layer.

QUESTION 24

Form of transmission in which signals are modulated as radiofrequency (RF) analog waves that use different frequency ranges:
    A. Baseline
    B. Baseband
    C. Midband
    D. Broadband

EXPLANATION

Broadband is the transmission system that carries RF signals across multiple channels on a coaxial cable, as used by cable TV.

QUESTION 25

In traditional broadband systems, signals travel in:
    A. two directions
    B. one direction
    C. more than one direction
    D. none of the above

EXPLANATION

In traditional broadband systems, signals travel toward the user. To allow users to send data as well, cable systems allot a separate channel space for the user's transmission and use amplifiers that can separate data the user issues from data the network transmits.

QUESTION 26

What do we call a network running more than one protocol?
    A. Single protocol network
    B. Unique protocol network
    C. Multiprotocol network
    D. Flexible protocol network

EXPLANATION

To manage a multiprotocol network, it is not only important to know about each protocol suite, but also to understand how they work together.

QUESTION 27

What can be said about TCP/IP?

    A. TCP/IP comprises several subprotocols

    B. TCP/IP comprises only one protocol

    C. TCP/IP has been replaced by ARP

    D. TCP/IP has been replaced by IPX/SPX

EXPLANATION

TCP/IP includes TCP, IP, UDP, ARP, and many other protocols.

QUESTION 28

For what network was TCP/IP first developed?

    A. Internet

    B. ARPAnet

    C. Ethernet

    D. WLAN

EXPLANATION

TCP/IP's roots lie with the U.S. Department of Defense, which developed TCP/IP for its Advanced Research Projects Agency network in the late 1960s.

QUESTION 29

Why has TCP/IP grown extremely popular?

    A. It is expensive

    B. It cannot be routable

    C. Its private nature made its programming code secure

    D. Its open nature

EXPLANATION

"Open" means that a software developer, for example, can use and modify TCP/IP's core protocols freely.

QUESTION 30

Where do the TCP/IP core protocols operate? (Choose 2)
- **A.** Session layer of the OSI Model
- **B.** Transport layer of the OSI Model
- **C.** Network layer of the OSI Model
- **D.** Application layer of the OSI Model

EXPLANATION

Certain subprotocols of the TCP/IP suite operate in the Transport and Network layers of the OSI Model and provide basic services to protocols in other layers.

QUESTION 31

Which are the most significant protocols in the TCP/IP suite? (Choose 2)
- **A.** TCP
- **B.** ARP
- **C.** IP
- **D.** UDP

EXPLANATION

TCP/IP core protocols operate in the Transport and Network layers of the OSI Model.

QUESTION 32

On what layer of the OSI Model does TCP operate?
- **A.** Physical
- **B.** Data Link
- **C.** Session
- **D.** Transport

EXPLANATION

TCP is part of the TCP/IP core protocols. TCP/IP core protocols operate in the Transport and Network layers of the OSI Model.

QUESTION 33

What can be said about TCP?

    A. It is a connectionless protocol

    B. It is a connection-oriented protocol

    C. TCP does not use checksums

    D. TCP does not ensure reliable data delivery

EXPLANATION

A connection must be established between communicating nodes before this protocol will transmit data.

QUESTION 34

What can be said about TCP?

    A. TCP does not use checksums

    B. It is a connectionless protocol

    C. TCP provides flow control

    D. TCP does not ensure reliable data delivery

EXPLANATION

TCP ensures that a node is not flooded with data.

QUESTION 35

The address on a host where an application makes itself available to incoming or outgoing data is also known as:

    A. IP address

    B. MAC address

    C. NIC address

    D. Port

EXPLANATION

One example of a port is port 80, which is typically used to accept Web page requests from the HTTP protocol.

QUESTION 36

On a TCP segment, what field indicates how many bytes the sender can issue to a receiver while acknowledgment for this segment is outstanding?

    A. Acknowledge number
    B. Window
    C. Reserved
    D. Checksum

EXPLANATION

Sliding-window size performs flow control, preventing the receiver from being deluged with bytes.

QUESTION 37

On a TCP segment, what field allows the receiving node to determine whether the TCP segment became corrupted during transmission?

    A. Checksum
    B. Flags
    C. TCP header length
    D. Padding

EXPLANATION

The Checksum field indicates the valid outcome of the error-checking algorithm used to verify the segment's header.

QUESTION 38

What is the only TCP/IP core protocol that runs at the Transport layer of the OSI Model?

    A. UDP
    B. IP
    C. TCP
    D. ARP

EXPLANATION

The Transmission Control Protocol (TCP) operates in the Transport layer of the OSI Model and provides reliable data delivery services.

QUESTION 39

This protocol that belongs to the Transport layer of the OSI Model is a connectionless transport service:

   A. TCP
   B. UDP
   C. IP
   D. HTTP

EXPLANATION

UDP offers no assurance that packets will be received in the correct sequence. In fact, this protocol does not guarantee that the packets will be received at all.

QUESTION 40

What can be said about UDP?

   A. TCP is more efficient than UDP
   B. UDP is more reliable than TCP
   C. UDP also uses checksums
   D. TCP produces more transmission overhead than UDP

EXPLANATION

UDP's lack of sophistication makes it more efficient than TCP.

QUESTION 41

How many header fields does UDP contain?

   A. 4
   B. 10
   C. 13
   D. 15

EXPLANATION

In contrast to a TCP header's 10 fields, the UDP header contains fewer fields.

QUESTION 42

To what layer of the OSI Model does the Internet Protocol (IP) belong?
- **A.** Network
- **B.** Transport
- **C.** Data Link
- **D.** Application

EXPLANATION

IP provides information about how and where data should be delivered, including the data's source and destination addresses.

QUESTION 43

What protocol allows TCP/IP to internetwork?
- **A.** TCP
- **B.** IP
- **C.** UDP
- **D.** ARP

EXPLANATION

IP is the subprotocol that enables TCP/IP to traverse more than one LAN segment and more than one type of network through a router.

QUESTION 44

In the context of TCP/IP, a packet is also known as:
- **A.** TCP/IP flow
- **B.** IP packet stream
- **C.** IP datagram
- **D.** TCP datagram

EXPLANATION

The IP datagram acts as an envelope for data and contains information necessary for routers to transfer data between different LAN segments.

QUESTION 45

What can be said about IP? (Choose 2)
- **A.** IP is a reliable protocol
- **B.** IP is an unreliable protocol
- **C.** IP is a connection-oriented protocol
- **D.** IP is a connectionless protocol

EXPLANATION

IP does not guarantee delivery of data.

QUESTION 46

What can be said about IP?
- **A.** IP is a reliable protocol
- **B.** IP operates a the Data Link layer of the OSI Model
- **C.** IP contains a header checksum field
- **D.** IP checksum also verifies the integrity of the message

EXPLANATION

The Header checksum verifies only the integrity of the routing information in the IP header.

QUESTION 47

What field of the IP datagram identifies the number of 4-byte (or 32-bit) blocks in the IP header?
- **A.** Flags
- **B.** Total length
- **C.** Version
- **D.** Internet Header Length

EXPLANATION

The IHL field is important because it indicates to the receiving node where data will begin (immediately after the header ends).

QUESTION 48

What field of the IP datagram informs routers what level of precedence they should apply when processing the incoming packet?

A. Differentiated Services
B. Total Length
C. Options
D. Flags

EXPLANATION

ToS specification allowed only eight different values regarding the precedence of a datagram. Differentiated Services allows for up to 64 values and a greater range of priority handling options.

QUESTION 49

What field of the IP datagram identifies the message to which a datagram belongs and enables the receiving node to reassemble fragmented messages?

A. Fragment Offset
B. Identification
C. Flags
D. Internet Header Length

EXPLANATION

Identification, Flags, and Fragment Offset fields assist in reassembly of fragmented packets.

QUESTION 50

What field of the IP datagram indicates the maximum time that a datagram can remain on the network before it is discarded?

A. Flags
B. Total Length
C. Time to Live
D. Options

EXPLANATION

Although the Time to Live field was originally meant to represent units of time, on modern networks it represents the number of times a datagram has been forwarded by a router, or the number of router hops it has endured.

QUESTION 51

Network layer protocol that reports on the success or failure of data delivery:

  A. IP
  B. TCP
  C. ARP
  D. ICMP

EXPLANATION

Internet Control Message Protocol can indicate when part of a network is congested, when data fails to reach its destination, and when data has been discarded because the allotted time for its delivery (its TTL) expired.

QUESTION 52

What can be said about ICMP?

  A. ICMP can correct detected errors
  B. ICMP identify and correct network errors
  C. ICMP cannot correct detected errors
  D. ICMP can correct but cannot identify network errors

EXPLANATION

ICMP announces transmission failures to the sender, but fixing functions is left to higher-layer protocols, such as TCP.

QUESTION 53

Network layer protocol that obtains the MAC (physical) address of a host, or node, then creates a database that maps the MAC address to the host's IP (logical) address:

  A. ARP
  B. UDP
  C. IP
  D. DNS

EXPLANATION

If one node needs to know the MAC address of another node on the same network, the first node issues a broadcast message to the network, using ARP, that essentially says, "Will the computer with the IP address 1.2.3.4 please send me its MAC address?"

QUESTION 54

What can be said about ARP?

A. ARP creates an ARP table for efficiency

B. ARP creates an ARP table for security

C. ARP does not create a MAC-to-IP table

D. ARP table and ARP cache are two completely different things

EXPLANATION

After a computer has saved this ARP information, the next time it needs the MAC address for another device, it will find the address in its ARP table and will not need to broadcast another request.

QUESTION 55

How many types of entries can an ARP table contain?

A. 1

B. 2

C. 3

D. 4

EXPLANATION

An ARP table can contain dynamic and static table entries.

QUESTION 56

ARP table entries that are created when a client makes an ARP request that cannot be satisfied by data already in the ARP table are know as:

A. Fixed entries

B. Static entries

C. New entries

D. Dynamic entries

EXPLANATION

Unlike dynamic ARP table entries, static ARP table entries are those that someone has entered manually using the ARP utility.

QUESTION 57

What is the name of the protocol that allows a client to send a broadcast message with its MAC address and receive an IP address in reply?

    A. ARP
    B. RARP
    C. DNS
    D. RDNS

EXPLANATION

This process is the reverse of ARP.

QUESTION 58

RARP was originally developed for:

    A. Full-fledged workstations
    B. Full clients
    C. Diskless workstations
    D. Servers

EXPLANATION

Diskless workstations are workstations that do not contain hard disks but rely on a small amount of read-only memory to connect to a network.

QUESTION 59

How many kinds of addresses does a network recognize?

    A. 2
    B. 3
    C. 4
    D. 5

EXPLANATION

Networks recognize logical (or Network layer) and physical (or MAC, or hardware) addresses.

QUESTION 60

What is the core protocol responsible for logical addressing for TCP/IP?

   A. MAC
   B. TCP
   C. ARP
   D. IP

EXPLANATION

Addresses on TCP/IP-based networks are often called IP addresses.

QUESTION 61

What is a valid IP address example?

   A. 144.92.43.178
   B. 144-92-43-178
   C. 144.92.43.1780
   D. 144,92,43,178

EXPLANATION

Each IP address is a unique 32-bit number, divided into four *octets*, or sets of 8 bits, that are separated by periods.

QUESTION 62

How many octets are in a valid IP address?

   A. 3
   B. 4
   C. 6
   D. 8

EXPLANATION

Each IP address is a unique 32-bit number, divided into four *octets*, or sets of 8 bits, that are separated by periods. Eight bits equals a byte.

QUESTION 63

How many types of information does an IP address contain?

    A. 1
    B. 2
    C. 3
    D. Unlimited

EXPLANATION

An IP address contains information about network and host.

QUESTION 64

How many types of networks classes are used on modern IP-based LANs?

    A. 1
    B. 2
    C. 3
    D. Unlimited

EXPLANATION

These are the types of network classes used on modern LANs: Class A, Class B, and Class C.

QUESTION 65

What type of transmission allows one device to send data to a specific group of devices (not necessarily the entire network segment)?

    A. Unicasting
    B. Broadcasting
    C. Multicasting
    D. Point-to-Point

EXPLANATION

Whereas most data transmission is on a point-to-point basis, multicasting is a point-to-multipoint method.

QUESTION 66

Although 8 bits have 256 possible combinations, to identify networks and hosts in an IP address you can use only numbers between:

   A. 0 and 255
   B. 1 and 254
   C. 2 and 256
   D. 125 and 256

EXPLANATION

For IP addressing, the number 0 is reserved to act as a placeholder when referring to an entire group of computers on a network and the number 255 is reserved for broadcast transmissions.

QUESTION 67

What IP address will you use to send a message to all devices connected to your network segment?

   A. 125.125.125.125
   B. 127.0.0.1
   C. 255.0.0.0
   D. 255.255.255.255

EXPLANATION

For IP addressing, the number 255 is reserved for broadcast transmissions.

QUESTION 68

To what network class does an IP address whose first octet is in the range of 1-126 belong?

   A. Class A
   B. Class B
   C. Class C
   D. Class D

EXPLANATION

All IP addresses for devices on a Class A segment share the same first octet, or bits 0 through 7.

QUESTION 69

In this example: 23.78.110.109, which one is the network ID?

A. 23
B. 78
C. 109
D. 110

EXPLANATION

The first octet represents the network ID and the second through fourth octets (bits 8 through 31) in a Class A address identify the host.

QUESTION 70

To what network class does an IP address whose first octet is in the range of 128–191 belong?

A. Class A
B. Class B
C. Class C
D. Class D

EXPLANATION

All IP addresses for devices on a Class B segment share the same first two octets, or bits 0 through 15.

QUESTION 71

In 168.34.88.29, which is the network ID?

A. 34.88
B. 34.88.29
C. 88.29
D. 168.34

EXPLANATION

The first two octets represent the network ID, and the third through fourth octets identify the host in a Class B address.

QUESTION 72

To what network class does an IP address whose first octet is in the range of 192-223 belong?

    A. Class A
    B. Class B
    C. Class C
    D. Class D

EXPLANATION

All IP addresses for devices on a Class C segment share the same first three octets, or bits 0 through 23.

QUESTION 73

In 204.139.118.7, which is the network ID?

    A. 7
    B. 118.7
    C. 139.118.7
    D. 204.139.118

EXPLANATION

The first three octets represent the network ID, and the fourth octet identifies the host in a Class C address.

QUESTION 74

Which of the following is a reason why IPv6 was originally developed?

    A. So that IP can operate at the Transport layer of the OSI Model
    B. To create a protocol that is not based on TCP
    C. To respond to an exponentially growing demand for IP addresses
    D. So that a network Class F can be used

EXPLANATION

IP version 6 (IPv6), also known as next-generation IP, will incorporate a new addressing scheme that can supply the world with enough addresses to last well into the Twenty-first century.

QUESTION 75

To what network class does the IP address 127.0.0.1 belong?

    A. Class A
    B. Class B
    C. Class C
    D. None of the above

EXPLANATION

Notice that 127 is not a valid first octet for any IP address.

QUESTION 76

The IP address 127.0.0.1 is also known as:

    A. Loopback address
    B. Broadcast address
    C. Multicast address
    D. Class B broadcast address

EXPLANATION

The range of addresses beginning with 127 is reserved for a device communicating with itself, or performing loopback communication.

QUESTION 77

What kind of IP address notation is address 131.65.10.18 using?

    A. Hexadecimal notation
    B. Dotted decimal notation
    C. Binary notation
    D. Octal notation

EXPLANATION

In dotted decimal notation, a decimal number between 0 and 255 represents each binary octet (for a total of 256 possibilities). A period, or dot, separates each decimal.

QUESTION 78

What kind of IP address notation is address 10000011 01000001 00001010 00100100 using?

- **A.** Hexadecimal notation
- **B.** Dotted decimal notation
- **C.** Binary notation
- **D.** Octal notation

EXPLANATION

The binary equivalent of "131" is 10000011, the binary equivalent of "65" is 01000001, the binary equivalent of "10" is 00001010, and the binary equivalent of "18" is 00100100.

QUESTION 79

A special 32-bit number that, when combined with a device's IP address, informs the rest of the network about the segment or network to which the device is attached:

- **A.** Subnet mask
- **B.** ARP address
- **C.** MAC address
- **D.** DNS mask

EXPLANATION

In addition to an IP address, every device on a TCP/IP-based network is identified by a subnet mask that informs the rest of the network about the segment or network to which the device is attached.

QUESTION 80

What can be said about subnet masks?

- **A.** They can be expressed using hexadecimal notation
- **B.** They are composed of four octets
- **C.** They are composed of three octets
- **D.** They can be expressed using octal notation

EXPLANATION

Like IP addresses, subnet masks are composed of four octets (32 bits) and can be expressed in either binary or dotted decimal notation.

QUESTION 81

What is the name of the process of subdividing a single class of network into multiple, smaller logical networks, or segments?

    A. Masking
    B. Segmentation
    C. Fragmentation
    D. Subnetting

EXPLANATION

Network managers create subnets to control network traffic and to make the best use of a limited number of IP addresses.

QUESTION 82

Which of the following statements is true?

    A. Subnet masks are assigned only to devices from a Class A network
    B. Devices are assigned a subnet mask only if they belong to a subnetted network
    C. Devices are always assigned a subnet mask
    D. Subnet masks are assigned only to devices from a Class A or B network

EXPLANATION

Whether or not a network is subnetted, its devices are assigned a subnet mask.

QUESTION 83

The mask 255.0.0.0 is the default subnet mask for what kind of network class?

    A. Class A
    B. Class B
    C. Class D
    D. Class E

EXPLANATION

If the beginning octets of the IP address are in the range 1–126, the default subnet mask will be 255.0.0.0.

QUESTION 84

The mask 255.255.0.0 is the default subnet mask for what kind of network class?
    A. Class A
    B. Class B
    C. Class C
    D. Class D

EXPLANATION

If the beginning octets of the IP address are in the range 128-191, the default subnet mask will be 255.255.0.0.

QUESTION 85

The mask 255.255.255.0 is the default subnet mask for what kind of network class?
    A. Class B
    B. Class C
    C. Class D
    D. Class E

EXPLANATION

If the beginning octets of the IP address are in the range 192-223, the default subnet mask will be 255.255.255.0.

QUESTION 86

What can be said about IP addresses within a LAN?
    A. Two devices can share the same IP address
    B. Exactly two devices can share an IP address at a time
    C. Exactly one device can use an IP address at a time
    D. Several devices can share the same IP address

EXPLANATION

Every node on a network must have a unique IP address.

QUESTION 87

What happens when you add a node to a network and its IP address is already in use by another node on the same subnet?

 A. Both hosts will stop working
 B. The new node will work, but the existing host will stop working
 C. They both will receive a message alert and stop working
 D. The existing host will continue working

EXPLANATION

In case of an IP address conflict, an error message will be generated on the new client, and its TCP/IP services will be disabled. The existing host may also receive an error message but can continue to function normally.

QUESTION 88

Manually assigned IP addresses are also known as:

 A. Static IP addresses
 B. Dynamic IP addresses
 C. Variable IP addresses
 D. Changing IP addresses

EXPLANATION

A static IP address does not change automatically. It changes only when you reconfigure the client's TCP/IP properties.

QUESTION 89

What type of IP address more easily results in the duplication of address assignments?

 A. Static IP addresses
 B. Dynamic IP addresses
 C. Variable IP addresses
 D. Changing IP addresses

EXPLANATION

Static addresses are vulnerable to human errors. Rather than assigning IP addresses manually, most network administrators rely on a network service to automatically assign them.

QUESTION 90

What is the name of the Application layer protocol that uses a central list of IP addresses and their associated devices' MAC addresses to assign IP addresses to clients dynamically?

    A. DHCP

    B. BOOTP

    C. DNSP

    D. DHCPP

EXPLANATION

When a client that relies on BOOTP first connects to the network, it sends a broadcast message to the network asking to be assigned an IP address. This broadcast message includes the MAC address of the client's NIC.

QUESTION 91

What information is included in a BOOTP response? (Choose 2)

    A. Client's hostname

    B. A default router's name

    C. IP address of the server

    D. IP address of a default router

EXPLANATION

The BOOTP server responds to the client with the following information: the client's IP address, the IP address of the server, the hostname of the server, and the IP address of a default router.

QUESTION 92

What can be said about BOOTP when compared to RARP?

    A. Both protocols are equal

    B. RARP is routable, while BOOTP is not

    C. BOOTP is routable, while RARP is not

    D. RARP is capable of sending more information to the client than BOOTP

EXPLANATION

If you wanted to use RARP to issue IP addresses, you would have to install a separate RARP server for every LAN. BOOTP, on the other hand, can traverse LANs.

QUESTION 93

What can be said about BOOTP when compared to DHCP?

A. DHCP requires less human intervention

B. BOOTP requires less human intervention

C. DHCP requires no human intervention, while BOOTP requires little human intervention

D. BOOTP requires no human intervention, while DHCP requires little human intervention

EXPLANATION

DHCP requires little intervention, whereas BOOTP requires network administrators to enter every IP and MAC address manually into the BOOTP table.

QUESTION 94

What is the name of the Application layer of the OSI Model protocol developed by the IETF as a replacement for BOOTP?

A. DNSP

B. DHCP

C. BOOTP+

D. RARP

EXPLANATION

Dynamic Host Configuration Protocol (DHCP) is an automated means of assigning a unique IP address to every device on a network. DHCP operates in a similar manner to BOOTP.

QUESTION 95

What is one benefit for implementing DHCP?

A. Keep users from moving their workstations without changing their TCP/IP configuration

B. Prevent mobile users from using your network

C. Reduce the time and planning spent on IP address management

D. None of the above

EXPLANATION

Central management of IP addresses eliminates the need for network administrators to edit the TCP/IP configuration on every network workstation, printer, or other device.

QUESTION 96

What can be said about DHCP when compared to BOOTP?
   A. DHCP is suitable for diskless workstations
   B. BOOTP is not suitable for diskless workstations
   C. DHCP is not suitable for diskless workstations
   D. Unlike BOOTP, DHCP requires no storage space

EXPLANATION

You may still encounter BOOTP in existing networks, but most likely it will support only diskless workstations, which are not capable of using DHCP.

QUESTION 97

What Transport layer protocol does a client use to broadcast a DHCP discover packet?
   A. ARP
   B. TCP
   C. IP
   D. UDP

EXPLANATION

When the client workstation is powered on and its NIC detects a network connection, it sends out a DHCP discover packet in broadcast fashion via the UDP protocol to the DHCP/BOOTP server.

QUESTION 98

What information is included in a DHCP response? (Choose 2)
   A. A default router's name
   B. IP address of the DHCP server
   C. A default router's IP address
   D. The lease duration

EXPLANATION

The response message includes the available IP address, subnet mask, IP address of the DHCP server, and the lease duration.

3

QUESTION 99

What is the next step a client will take upon receiving responses from all DHCP servers on the client's subnet?

A. The client accepts all IP addresses it receives

B. The client accepts only one IP address

C. The client accepts two IP address

D. The client accepts the last IP address it receives

EXPLANATION

The client accepts the first IP address that it receives, responding with a broadcast message that essentially confirms to the DHCP server that it wants to accept the address.

QUESTION 100

How many packet exchanges does DHCP comprise?

A. Exactly one

B. Less than three

C. Less than six

D. More than 7

EXPLANATION

DHCP involves the exchange of only four packets and therefore does not usually increase the time it takes for a client to log on to the network.

QUESTION 101

What is the Windows XP command to release an old DHCP lease?

A. ipconfig /release

B. ifconfig /release

C. netstat /release

D. ipconfig /renew

EXPLANATION

On a Windows XP operating system, at the command prompt, type ipconfig /release and then press Enter. Your TCP/IP configuration values will be cleared, and both the IP address and subnet mask will revert to 0.0.0.0.

QUESTION 102

What is the Windows XP command to obtain a new IP address?

A. ipconfig /renew

B. ifconfig /renew

C. netstat /release

D. ipconfig /release

EXPLANATION

On a Windows XP operating system, at the command prompt, type ipconfig /renew and then press Enter. Your client follows the DHCP leasing process, which reestablishes its TCP/IP configuration values.

QUESTION 103

What is the name of the protocol developed by Microsoft to address the possibility that a computer might be configured to use DHCP but be unable to find a DHCP server?

A. ARIPA

B. IANA

C. RARP

D. APIPA

EXPLANATION

Microsoft offers Automatic Private IP Addressing for its Windows 98, Me, 2000, XP Client, and Windows 2003 Server operating systems.

QUESTION 104

To what network class does APIPA pool of addresses belong?

A. Class A

B. Class B

C. Class C

D. Class D

EXPLANATION

APIPA assigns the computer's network adapter an IP address from a predefined pool of addresses, 169.254.0.0 through 169.254.255.255.

QUESTION 105

What subnet mask does APIPA use?

    A. 255.0.0.0

    B. 255.0.255.0.0

    C. 255.255.0.0

    D. 255.255.255.0

EXPLANATION

APIPA assigns the default subnet mask for a Class B network.

QUESTION 106

What can be said about APIPA regarding DHCP?

    A. Once a client obtains an APIPA address, it cannot apply for a DHCP lease

    B. A client with an APIPA address has to wait 30 minutes before applying for a DHCP lease

    C. A client with an APIPA address can apply for a DHCP lease and use both IP addresses with the same NIC

    D. None of the above

EXPLANATION

In the case of a network whose DHCP is temporarily unavailable, when the DHCP server is available once again, APIPA will release its assigned IP address and allow the client to receive a DHCP-assigned address.

QUESTION 107

After APIPA assigns an address, a computer can:

    A. Communicate with any other node across a LAN

    B. Communicate with a limited set of nodes across a LAN

    C. Communicate with other subnets

    D. Communicate with the APIPA server only

EXPLANATION

After APIPA assigns an address, a computer can then communicate across a LAN. However, it can communicate only with other nodes using addresses in the APIPA range.

QUESTION 108

What can be said of a client using an APIPA-assigned address?

    A. It cannot send or receive data to or from the Internet

    B. It can communicate with nodes on other subnets

    C. It can communicate with any other WAN

    D. It can send or receive data to or from any WAN

EXPLANATION

It cannot communicate with nodes on other subnets.

QUESTION 109

What command can be used on a Windows XP operating system to find out if the client has APIPA enabled?

    A. ipconf /apipa-enabled

    B. ifconfig /all

    C. ipconfig /all

    D. iplease /apipa

EXPLANATION

On a Windows XP computer, at the command prompt, type ipconfig /all and then press Enter. If the Autoconfiguration Enabled option is set to Yes, your computer is using APIPA.

QUESTION 110

What is true about APIPA?

    A. APIPA will overwrite manually assigned IP addresses

    B. Leaving APIPA enable is always problematic

    C. APIPA cannot be disabled

    D. It works only with clients configured to use DHCP

EXPLANATION

APIPA is designed to check for the presence of a DHCP server and allow the DHCP server to assign addresses.

QUESTION 111

A port number can be compared to:

A. A building address

B. An apartment number on a building

C. A building number

D. An intersection of two streets

EXPLANATION

If you compare IP addressing with the addressing system used by the postal service, and you equate a host's IP address to the address of a building, a port number would be similar to an apartment number within that building.

QUESTION 112

A process' socket is equal to:

A. Port number + IP address

B. IP address

C. Port number

D. IP address + hostname + port number

EXPLANATION

A process's port number plus its host machine's IP address equals the process's *socket*.

QUESTION 113

How would you represent a Telnet port on a host with IP address 10.43.3.87?

A. 10.43.3.87:80

B. 10.43.3.87:23

C. 10.43.3.87:33

D. 10.43.3.87:21

EXPLANATION

A port number is expressed as a number following a colon after an IP address.

QUESTION 114

A virtual connection between a process on one computer and the same process running on another computer is also known as:
- **A.** Routing
- **B.** VPN
- **C.** Tunneling
- **D.** Socket

EXPLANATION

Sockets form virtual connections between a process on one computer and the same process running on another computer.

QUESTION 115

Select one benefit in using port numbers:
- **A.** Makes TCP/IP more complicated
- **B.** Increases security
- **C.** Ensures that data is transmitted to the correct application
- **D.** Increases the number of IP addresses required

EXPLANATION

When a client requests communications with a server and specifies port 23, for example, the server knows immediately that the client wants a Telnet session.

QUESTION 116

Select an appropriate port number: (Choose 2)
- **A.** 1,024
- **B.** 62,334
- **C.** 65,700
- **D.** 69,000

EXPLANATION

Port numbers range from 0 to 65,535.

QUESTION 117

How many types of port numbers are there according to IANA?

A. 1
B. 2
C. 3
D. 4

EXPLANATION

Port numbers are divided by IANA into three types: Well Known Ports, Registered Ports, and Dynamic and/or Private Ports.

QUESTION 118

Select an appropriate Well Known port number:

A. 1020
B. 2500
C. 3345
D. 3789

EXPLANATION

Well Known ports are in the range of 0 to 1023.

QUESTION 119

What type of port number does TCP use?

A. Private port
B. Dynamic port
C. Registered port
D. Well Known port

EXPLANATION

The earliest TCP/IP protocols use Well Known ports.

QUESTION 120

Select an appropriate Registered port number:
- **A.** 512
- **B.** 698
- **C.** 47,568
- **D.** 67,896

EXPLANATION

Registered ports are in the range of 1,024 to 49,151.

3

QUESTION 121

Select an appropriate Dynamic and/or Private port number:
- **A.** 12,398
- **B.** 39,337
- **C.** 45,152
- **D.** 63,456

EXPLANATION

Dynamic and/or Private ports are those from 49,152 through 65,535.

QUESTION 122

Port numbers of this type do not need to be registered with IANA in order to use them:
- **A.** Well Know port
- **B.** Registered port
- **C.** Dynamic and/or Private port
- **D.** TCP port

EXPLANATION

Dynamic and/or Private ports are open for use without restriction.

QUESTION 123

Select one advantage of IPv6:

A. Requires new network equipment

B. Better security

C. Bigger header

D. All of the above

EXPLANATION

IPv6 offers a more efficient header, better security, and better prioritization allowances than IPv4, plus automatic IP address configuration.

QUESTION 124

With respect to IPv4, how many more IP addresses can be used with IPv6?

A. 2^{23}

B. 2^{36}

C. 2^{63}

D. 2^{96}

EXPLANATION

The added fields and the larger address size result in an increase of 4 billion times 4 billion times 4 billion available IP addresses in the IPv6 addressing scheme.

QUESTION 125

What is the correct representation of an IPv6 address?

A. Binary numbers separated by a period

B. Hexadecimal numbers separated by a colon

C. Decimal numbers separated by a period

D. Decimal numbers separated by a colon

EXPLANATION

An example of a valid IPv6 address is F:F:0:0:0:0:3012:0CE3.

QUESTION 126

What does the shorthand representation of IPv6 specify?

A. Substitute "::" for any number of multiple, zero-value fields

B. Substitute ":" for any number of multiple, zero-value fields

C. Substitute ".." for any number of multiple, zero-value fields

D. Substitute ";;" for any number of multiple, zero-value fields

EXPLANATION

An example of a valid IPv6 address is F:F:0:0:0:0:3012:0CE3. The IPv6 address example could be also written as F:F::3012:0CE3.

QUESTION 127

Recall that in IPv4 the loopback address has a value of 127.0.0.1. What is the loopback address for IPv6?

A. F:F:0:0:0:0:3012:0CE3

B. F:0:F:0:F:0:F:1

C. 0:0:0:0:0:0:0:1

D. F:F:0:0:0:0:0:0:0:1

EXPLANATION

Abbreviated, the IPv6 loopback address becomes ::1.

QUESTION 128

How many types of network interfaces can IPv6 distinguish?

A. 2

B. 3

C. 4

D. 5

EXPLANATION

IPv6 addressing can distinguish between unicast, multicast, and anycast interfaces.

QUESTION 129

On IPv6, what is the name for an address that represents a single interface on a device?

A. Broadcast

B. Multicast

C. Anycast

D. Unicast

EXPLANATION

A unicast address is the type of address that would be assigned, for example, to a workstation's network adapter.

QUESTION 130

On IPv6, what is the name for an address that represents multiple interfaces (often on multiple devices)?

A. Broadcast

B. Multicast

C. Anycast

D. Unicast

EXPLANATION

Multicast addresses are useful for transmitting the same data to many different devices simultaneously.

QUESTION 131

On IPv6, what is the name for an address that represents any one interface from a group of interfaces (often on multiple nodes), any one of which (usually the first available) can accept a transmission?

A. Broadcast

B. Multicast

C. Anycast

D. Unicast

EXPLANATION

Anycast addresses could be useful for identifying all of the routers that belong to one ISP, for example. In this instance, an Internet transmission destined for one of that ISP's servers could be accepted by the first available router in the anycast group.

QUESTION 132

At this time, to what type of network components can anycast addresses be assigned?
- **A.** Routers
- **B.** Hosts
- **C.** Servers
- **D.** Workstations

EXPLANATION

At this time, anycast addresses are not designed to be assigned to hosts, such as servers or workstations.

QUESTION 133

What is the name of a variable-length field at the beginning of a IPv6 address that indicates what type of address it is?
- **A.** Broadcast Prefix
- **B.** Format Prefix
- **C.** Format Suffix
- **D.** Unicast Suffix

EXPLANATION

In IPv6, the first field of the IP address would provide a clue as to what type of interface the address represented. The Format Prefix also establishes the arrangement of the rest of the address's fields.

QUESTION 134

What types of IPv6 addresses begins with the hexadecimal string FEC0? (Choose two)
- **A.** Broadcast
- **B.** Unicast
- **C.** Multicast
- **D.** Anycast

EXPLANATION

A unicast or anycast address begins with one of the two following hexadecimal strings: FEC0 or FE80.

QUESTION 135

A name that describes the device on a network is also known as:

    A. Hostname

    B. IP name

    C. IP address

    D. Socket

EXPLANATION

Every device on the Internet is technically known as a host. Every host can take a hostname. For example, someone named Peggy McDonald might name her workstation "Peggy."

QUESTION 136

A group of computers that belong to the same organization and have part of their IP addresses in common is also known as:

    A. Hostname

    B. Domain

    C. Host bastion

    D. Server room

EXPLANATION

A domain is identified by its domain name. Usually, a domain name is associated with a company or other type of organization, such as a university, government organization, or company.

QUESTION 137

What does a fully qualified hostname comprise?

    A. Hostname

    B. Domain name

    C. Hostname + domain name

    D. IP Address + Socket

EXPLANATION

If you worked at the Library of Congress and gave your workstation the hostname Peggy, your fully qualified hostname might be Peggy.loc.gov.

QUESTION 138

A domain name is represented by a series of:
- **A.** Decimal numbers separated by dots
- **B.** Binary numbers separated by dots
- **C.** Labels separated by colons
- **D.** Labels separated by dots

EXPLANATION

A domain name is represented by a series of character strings, separated by dots.

QUESTION 139

What does a label represent on a domain name?
- **A.** A level in the domain naming hierarchy
- **B.** A part of the organization name
- **C.** A part of the organization IP address
- **D.** None of the above

EXPLANATION

In the domain name *www.novell.com*, *com* is the top-level domain (TLD), *novell* is the second-level domain, and *www* is the third-level domain.

QUESTION 140

How many third level domains can a second level domain contain?
- **A.** Only 1
- **B.** Less than 3
- **C.** Exactly 3
- **D.** Several

EXPLANATION

For instance, in addition to www.novell.com, Novell also owns the following domains: support.novell.com, developer.novell.com, and ftp.novell.com.

QUESTION 141

Domain names must be registered with this organization or an Internet naming authority that works on behalf of it:

    A. IETF

    B. ICANN

    C. ISO

    D. ANSI

EXPLANATION

ICANN has established conventions for domain naming so that certain TLDs apply to every type of organization that uses the Internet.

QUESTION 142

Besides the popular .com, .org and .net, ICANN has approved these others Top-Level Domains (TLD): (Choose 2)

    A. .ca

    B. .museums

    C. .jp

    D. .pros

EXPLANATION

ICANN has approved over 240 country code TLDs to represent different countries and territories across the globe.

QUESTION 143

A hierarchical way of associating domain names with IP addresses is known as:

    A. ARP

    B. DNS

    C. RARP

    D. IP

EXPLANATION

"DNS" refers to both the Application layer service that accomplishes name association with IP address and also the organized system of computers and databases that makes this association possible.

QUESTION 144

What are some of the advantages of DNS? (Choose 2)

    A. Distributed

    B. Resilient to a handful of servers experiencing errors

    C. Secure

    D. Flat organization

EXPLANATION

The DNS service does not rely on one file or even one server, but rather on many computers across the globe.

QUESTION 145

How many components does a DNS include?

    A. 1

    B. 2

    C. 3

    D. 4

EXPLANATION

To direct traffic efficiently, the DNS service is divided into three components: resolvers, name servers, and name space.

QUESTION 146

Select two Application layer protocols used to send and receive files via TCP/IP: (Choose 2)

    A. Telnet

    B. FTP

    C. NTP

    D. TFTP

EXPLANATION

FTP and TFTP enable clients to transfer files between computers. The main difference is that FTP uses TCP, while TFTP uses UDP as a transport protocol.

QUESTION 147

What does NTP stand for?
- **A.** News Transfer Protocol
- **B.** News Transport Protocol
- **C.** Network Time Protocol
- **D.** Name Transport Protocol

EXPLANATION

The Network Time Protocol (NTP) is a simple Application layer protocol used to synchronize the clocks of computers on a network.

QUESTION 148

Where do the most significant IPX/SPX core protocols operate with respect to the OSI Model? (Choose 2)
- **A.** Network Layer
- **B.** Application Layer
- **C.** Session Layer
- **D.** Transport Layer

EXPLANATION

IPX operates at the Network layer of the OSI Model, and SPX belongs to the Transport layer of the OSI Model.

QUESTION 149

How many connections can NetBEUI support?
- **A.** Less than 300
- **B.** More than 300
- **C.** Exactly 300
- **D.** Exactly 552

EXPLANATION

NetBEUI can support only 254 connections.

QUESTION 150

What is the name of the service that provides a means of resolving NetBIOS names to IP addresses?

    A. NetBEUI

    B. NetDNS

    C. WINS

    D. MSDNS

EXPLANATION

WINS is used exclusively with systems that use NetBIOS. WINS has the same relationship to NetBIOS as DNS has to TCP/IP.

QUESTION 151

What is the name of the protocol suite originally designed to interconnect Macintosh computers?

    A. IPforMAC

    B. AppleTalk

    C. MacBIOS

    D. AppleNet

EXPLANATION

Although AppleTalk was meant to support peer-to-peer networking among Macintoshes, it can be routed between network segments and integrated with NetWare-, UNIX-, Linux-, or Microsoft-based networks.

QUESTION 152

Which of the following is not a method for switching?

    A. Circuit

    B. Message

    C. Network

    D. Packet

EXPLANATION

These are the methods for switching: circuit switching, message switching, and packet switching.

QUESTION 153

What is the name of the switching method where a connection is established between two network nodes before they begin transmitting data?

- **A.** Message switching
- **B.** Packet switching
- **C.** Network switching
- **D.** Circuit switching

EXPLANATION

In circuit switching, connection bandwidth is dedicated to this connection and remains available until the users terminate communication between the two nodes.

QUESTION 154

What is the name of the switching method where a connection is established between two devices, transfers the information to the second device, and then breaks the connection?

- **A.** Message switching
- **B.** Packet switching
- **C.** Network switching
- **D.** Circuit switching

EXPLANATION

In message switching, all information follows the same physical path; unlike with circuit switching, however, the connection is not continuously maintained.

QUESTION 155

What is the name of the switching method that breaks data into packets before they are transported?

- **A.** Message switching
- **B.** Packet switching
- **C.** Network switching
- **D.** Circuit switching

EXPLANATION

In packet switching, packets can travel any path on the network to their destination because each packet contains the destination address and sequencing information.

QUESTION 156

What are two benefits of FDDI?

A. Reliability

B. Cost

C. Security

D. The use of copper-based wiring

EXPLANATION

Its reliance on fiber-optic cable ensures that FDDI is more reliable and more secure than transmission methods that depend on copper wiring. Another advantage of FDDI is that it works well with Ethernet 100BASE-TX technology.

QUESTION 157

What term from the following list refers to the network of typical telephone lines and carrier equipment that service most homes?

A. Ethernet

B. WAN

C. Mesh

D. PSTN

EXPLANATION

The PSTN comprises the entire telephone system, from the lines that connect homes and businesses to the network centers that connect different regions of a country.

QUESTION 158

Since not all of the PSTN is capable of handling digital transmission, what kind of device is required at both ends of the communication?

A. Router

B. Modem

C. Switch

D. Access point

EXPLANATION

A modem converts a computer's digital pulses into analog signals before it issues them to the telephone line and then converts the analog signals back into digital pulses at the receiving computer's end.

QUESTION 159

What is the most limiting disadvantage of PSTN?

A. Quality

B. Security

C. Speed

D. Limited number of central offices

EXPLANATION

PSTN comes with significant disadvantages. Most limiting is its low throughput. Currently, manufacturers of PSTN modems advertise a connection speed of 56 Kbps.

QUESTION 160

On what kind of switching technology does X.25 rely?

A. Packet switching

B. Message switching

C. Network switching

D. Circuit switching

EXPLANATION

X.25 is an analog, packet-switched technology designed for long-distance data transmission and standardized by the ITU in the mid-1970s.

ANSWER GRID FOR DOMAIN 2

Question	Answer	Objective	Question	Answer	Objective
1	C	2.2	16	C	2.2
2	D	2.2	17	D	2.2
3	A	2.2	18	B	2.2
4	B	2.2	19	A	2.1
5	C	2.2	20	B	2.1
6	A	2.2	21	C	2.1
7	B	2.2	22	A	2.2
8	D	2.2	23	B	2.3
9	C	2.2	24	D	2.15
10	C	2.2	25	B	2.15
11	D	2.2	26	C	2.4
12	A	2.2	27	A	2.4
13	B	2.2	28	B	2.4
14	A	2.3	29	D	2.4
15	D	2.3	30	B, C	2.4

Question	Answer	Objective	Question	Answer	Objective
31	A, C	2.4	71	D	2.4, 2,5, 2.6
32	D	2.10	72	C	2.4, 2,5, 2.6
33	B	2.10	73	D	2.4, 2,5, 2.6
34	C	2.10	74	C	2.4, 2,5, 2.6
35	D	2.10	75	D	2.4, 2,5, 2.6
36	B	2.10	76	A	2.4, 2,5, 2.6
37	A	2.10	77	B	2.5
38	C	2.4	78	C	2.5
39	B	2.10	79	A	2.4, 2.6, 2.7
40	D	2.10	80	B	2.4, 2.6, 2.7
41	A	2.10	81	D	2.4, 2.6, 2.7
42	A	2.4	82	C	2.4, 2.6, 2.7
43	B	2.4	83	A	2.4, 2.6, 2.7
44	C	2.4	84	B	2.4, 2.6, 2.7
45	B, D	2.4	85	B	2.4, 2.6, 2.7
46	C	2.4	86	C	2.4, 2.5, 2.9
47	D	2.5	87	D	2.4, 2.5, 2.9
48	A	2.5	88	A	2.4, 2.5, 2.9
49	B	2.5	89	A	2.4, 2.5, 2.9
50	C	2.5	90	B	2.4, 2.5, 2.9
51	D	2.10	91	C, D	2.4, 2.5, 2.9
52	C	2.10	92	C	2.4, 2.5, 2.9
53	A	2.10	93	A	2.4, 2.5, 2.9
54	A	2.10	94	B	2.4, 2.5, 2.9
55	B	2.10	95	C	2.4, 2.5, 2.9
56	D	2.10	96	C	2.4, 2.5, 2.9
57	B	2.10	97	D	2.4, 2.5, 2.9
58	C	2.10	98	B, D	2.4, 2.5, 2.9
59	A	2.4	99	B	2.4, 2.5, 2.9
60	D	2.4	100	C	2.4, 2.5, 2.9
61	A	2.4	101	A	2.4, 2.5, 2.9
62	B	2.4, 2,5, 2.6	102	A	2.4, 2.5, 2.9
63	B	2.4, 2,5, 2.6	103	D	2.4, 2.5, 2.9
64	C	2.4, 2,5, 2.6	104	B	2.4, 2.5, 2.9
65	C	2.4, 2,5, 2.6	105	C	2.4, 2.5, 2.9
66	B	2.4, 2,5, 2.6	106	D	2.4, 2.5, 2.9
67	D	2.4, 2,5, 2.6	107	B	2.4, 2.5, 2.9
68	A	2.4, 2,5, 2.6	108	A	2.4, 2.5, 2.9
69	A	2.4, 2,5, 2.6	109	C	2.4, 2.5, 2.9
70	B	2.4, 2,5, 2.6	110	D	2.4, 2.5, 2.9

3

Question	Answer	Objective	Question	Answer	Objective
111	B	2.11, 2.12	136	B	2.13
112	A	2.11, 2.12	137	C	2.13
113	B	2.11, 2.12	138	D	2.13
114	D	2.11, 2.12	139	A	2.13
115	C	2.11, 2.12	140	D	2.13
116	A, B	2.11, 2.12	141	B	2.13
117	C	2.11, 2.12	142	A, C	2.13
118	A	2.11, 2.12	143	B	2.13
119	D	2.11, 2.12	144	A, B	2.13
120	C	2.11, 2.12	145	C	2.13
121	D	2.11, 2.12	146	B, D	2.10
122	C	2.11, 2.12	147	C	2.10
123	B	2.4, 2.5	148	A, D	2.4
124	D	2.4, 2.5	149	A	2.4
125	B	2.4, 2.5	150	C	2.13
126	A	2.4, 2.5	151	B	2.4
127	C	2.4, 2.5	152	C	2.14
128	B	2.4, 2.5	153	D	2.14
129	D	2.4, 2.5	154	A	2.14
130	B	2.4, 2.5	155	B	2.14
131	C	2.4, 2.5	156	A, C	2.14
132	A	2.4, 2.5	157	D	2.15
133	B	2.4, 2.5	158	B	2.15
134	B, D	2.4, 2.5	159	C	2.15
135	A	2.13	160	A	2.14

4

DOMAIN 3: NETWORK IMPLEMENTATION

All questions in this chapter pertain to Domain 3, Network Implementation, of the CompTIA Network+® exam. This domain represents 25% of the total exam and has 12 sub-objectives.

For more in-depth information about this domain, see Appendix A, "Network+ (2005) Examination Objectives."

QUESTION 1

A computer on the network that requests resources or services from another computer on a network:

    A. Server

    B. Connectivity device

    C. Client

    D. Database server

EXPLANATION

The term "client" may also refer to the human user of a client workstation or to client software installed on the workstation.

QUESTION 2

A computer on the network that manages shared resources:

    A. Client

    B. Server

    C. Workstation

    D. Client software

EXPLANATION

Servers run network operating software that can manage not only data, but also users, groups, security, and applications on the network.

QUESTION 3

A personal computer (such as a desktop or laptop), which may or may not be connected to a network:

A. Workstation
B. Server
C. Client
D. DNS server

EXPLANATION

Most clients are workstation computers.

QUESTION 4

The software that runs on a server and enables the server to manage data, users, groups, security, applications, and other networking functions:

A. Database client
B. Agent
C. Client
D. Network operating system (NOS)

EXPLANATION

The most popular network operating systems are Microsoft Windows Server 2003, Novell NetWare, UNIX, and Linux.

QUESTION 5

A specialized device that allows multiple networks or multiple parts of one network to connect and exchange data:

A. Antenna
B. Transceiver
C. Receiver
D. Connectivity device

EXPLANATION

A client/server network can operate without connectivity devices. However, medium and large-sized LANs use them to extend the network and to connect with WANs.

QUESTION 6

A part of a network is also known as:

A. LAN
B. segment
C. Ethernet
D. route

EXPLANATION

Usually, a segment comprises a group of nodes that use the same communications channel for all their traffic.

4

QUESTION 7

What is the name for the part of a network to which segments and significant shared devices (such as routers, switches, and servers) connect?

A. Router
B. Telco room
C. Backbone
D. Main line

EXPLANATION

A backbone is sometimes referred to as "a network of networks" because of its role in interconnecting smaller parts of a LAN or WAN.

QUESTION 8

What is the name for any standard method or format for communication between networked devices?

A. Protocol
B. IEEE standard
C. IETF standard
D. Structured cabling

EXPLANATION

Protocols ensure that data is transferred whole, in sequence, and without error from one node on the network to another.

QUESTION 9

What is the name for the distinct units of data that are transmitted from one node on a network to another?

A. Protocols
B. Network operating systems
C. Data packets
D. Signals

EXPLANATION

Breaking a large stream of data into many packets allows a network to deliver that data more efficiently and reliably.

QUESTION 10

The scheme for assigning a unique identifying number to every node on the network:

A. Identification
B. Addressing
C. Logging
D. Transport

EXPLANATION

The type of addressing used depends on the network's protocols and network operating system.

QUESTION 11

What operating system requires a protocol suite binding process?

A. UNIX
B. Linux
C. BSD
D. Windows XP

EXPLANATION

UNIX and Linux only support the TCP/IP protocol suite, and the TCP/IP protocols are automatically bound to the network interface (or interfaces).

QUESTION 12

What is the name for the process of assigning one network component to work with another?

A. Burning

B. Binding

C. Attaching

D. Registering

EXPLANATION

You can manually bind protocols that are not already associated with a network interface.

4

QUESTION 13

What can be said about the binding protocol process?

A. It is not possible to bind the same protocols on multiple network adapters

B. It is not possible to bind multiple protocols to the same network adapter

C. It is possible to bind multiple protocols to the same network adapter

D. All of the above

EXPLANATION

Binding multiple protocols is necessary on networks that use more than one type of protocol.

QUESTION 14

What is one of the most limiting factors when choosing a network operating system (NOS)?

A. Existing infrastructure

B. Internet connection

C. Broadband connection

D. Popularity of your choice

EXPLANATION

When choosing a NOS, your decision will probably depend largely on the operating systems and applications already running on the LAN.

QUESTION 15

What is one of the most important factors when choosing the hardware for your network servers?

    A. NOS
    B. Internet connection
    C. Hardware brand
    D. Application requirements

EXPLANATION

Perhaps the most important question in this list involves the types of applications to be run by the server.

QUESTION 16

What is one of the most important functions provided by a NOS?

    A. Internet connection
    B. Client support
    C. Security
    D. All of the above

EXPLANATION

The primary reason for using networks is to enable clients to communicate and share resources efficiently.

QUESTION 17

What is the name of the software that translates requests and responses between the client and server?

    A. Hardware
    B. Centerware
    C. Middleware
    D. Transware

EXPLANATION

Middleware stands in the middle of the client and the server and performs some of the tasks that an application in a simple client/server relationship would otherwise perform.

QUESTION 18

To manage network access more easily, you can combine users with similar needs and restrictions into:

A. Sections
B. Areas
C. Categories
D. Groups

EXPLANATION

In every NOS, groups form the basis for resource and account management. Many network administrators create groups according to department or, even more specifically, according to job function within a department.

4

QUESTION 19

What is the name used by an NOS for a list that organizes resources and associates them with their characteristics?

A. Directory
B. Client software
C. File list
D. Resources list

EXPLANATION

One example of a directory is a file system directory, which organizes files and their characteristics, such as file size, owner, type, and permissions.

QUESTION 20

What term defines the ability of a processor to perform many different operations in a very brief period of time?

A. Efficiency
B. Multitasking
C. Parallel processing
D. Multiprocessing

EXPLANATION

If you have used multiple programs on a desktop computer, you have taken advantage of your operating system's multitasking capability.

QUESTION 21

What is true about Microsoft Windows Server 2003?

A. Can interact with any kind of client

B. Can interact with almost any kind of client

C. Can interact only with Microsoft clients

D. Can interact only with Microsoft clients 2003 or higher

EXPLANATION

Microsoft Windows Server 2003 can communicate with almost any kind of client.

QUESTION 22

What application should be installed to allow Microsoft Windows Server 2003 to communicate with NetWare Server version 5.x or 6.x?

A. File and Print Client for NetWare

B. File and Print Server for NetWare

C. File and Print Services for NetWare

D. All of the above

EXPLANATION

File and Print Services for NetWare is one application belonging to the Microsoft Windows Services for NetWare package, a collection of software that simplifies the integration of Windows Server 2003 servers and NetWare servers on the same network.

QUESTION 23

What application should be installed to synchronize information between an Active Directory database and a NetWare directory database?

A. Microsoft Directory Synchronization Services

B. NetWare Directory Synchronization Services

C. Microsoft-NetWare Synchronization Server

D. Synchronization Client for NetWare on Windows Server

EXPLANATION

Another application that belongs to the Microsoft Windows Services for NetWare package is the Microsoft Directory Synchronization Services (MSDSS).

QUESTION 24

What application can NetWare clients relying on IPX/SPX install to access Microsoft Windows Server 2003?

- **A.** Microsoft's Server for NetWare
- **B.** Client Services for NetWare
- **C.** Microsoft Windows Services for NetWare
- **D.** NetWare Connection Tools

EXPLANATION

For NetWare clients that rely on the IPX/SPX protocol, additional software is necessary to access a Windows Server 2003 server. One possibility is for clients that depend on the Windows Server 2003 server to run Microsoft's Client Services for NetWare (CSNW).

4

QUESTION 25

What is the name of the set of applications that allows UNIX-based clients to connect to Windows Server 2003?

- **A.** UNIX2Windows Client
- **B.** Windows Server Client for UNIX
- **C.** UNIX Services for Windows
- **D.** Windows Services for UNIX

EXPLANATION

Windows Services for UNIX is installed on the Windows server and allows clients attached to the UNIX type of server to access Windows Server 2003 resources as if they were resources on the UNIX type of server.

QUESTION 26

What is the name of the set of applications that allows clients on Windows Server 2003 to connect to a UNIX-type server?

- **A.** Windows Services for UNIX
- **B.** UNIX Services for Windows
- **C.** UNIX Server for Windows
- **D.** Windows2UNIX Client

EXPLANATION

Another application belonging to the Windows Services for UNIX package allows clients on Windows Server 2003 networks to access UNIX-type servers and use their files and account privileges.

QUESTION 27

What protocol suite did NetWare originally use?

    A. NetBios

    B. TCP/IP

    C. IPX/SPX

    D. UDP

EXPLANATION

NetWare versions prior to 4.11 require the IPX/SPX protocol suite. With 4.11, the version sometimes referred to as *intraNetWare*, NetWare began supporting TCP/IP.

QUESTION 28

What kind of hard disk partition does a NetWare 6.5 server need?

    A. ext2

    B. DOS

    C. NTFS

    D. ext3

EXPLANATION

NetWare kernel is started by the program server.exe, which runs from a server's DOS partition (over the DOS operating system) when a server boots up.

QUESTION 29

How many processors does NetWare 6.5 support?

    A. 4

    B. 8

    C. 16

    D. 32

EXPLANATION

In versions 4.x and higher, NetWare supports the use of as many as 32 processors on one server.

QUESTION 30

What does NLM stand for?

A. NetWare Loadable Module
B. Network Level Manager
C. NetWare List Memory
D. NetWare Level Memory

EXPLANATION

NLMs are routines that enable the server to run a range of programs and offer a variety of services. The NetWare Integrated Kernel is responsible for loading and unloading them.

4

QUESTION 31

What is the preferred filesystem in NetWare 6.5?

A. NTFS
B. FAT
C. NSS
D. ext2

EXPLANATION

NSS (Novell Storage Services) is selected by default during NetWare 6.5 installation.

QUESTION 32

What is the minimum number of partitions that a NetWare 6.5 server requires?

A. 1
B. 2
C. 3
D. 4

EXPLANATION

The DOS partition is the primary boot partition, from which the server.exe file runs. At least one additional partition must be present to hold the NetWare program and data files.

QUESTION 33

What is a unique feature of NSS?

 A. Volumes
 B. Organizes information into files and directories
 C. Files or directories as large as 8 Megabytes (MB)
 D. Storage pools

EXPLANATION

One unique feature of NSS is the ability to combine free storage space from multiple hard disks or other storage devices, such as CDs.

QUESTION 34

How many access categories does NetWare 6.5 provide for clients to access the server and its resources?

 A. 2
 B. 3
 C. 4
 D. 5

EXPLANATION

Access methods can be categorized as follows: traditional client access, native file access, and browser-based access.

QUESTION 35

What access category did a Windows client traditionally use in NetWare?

 A. Browser-based access
 B. Native file access
 C. Traditional client access
 D. NetWare access

EXPLANATION

In previous versions of NetWare, clients running Windows, Macintosh, and UNIX-type operating systems traditionally connected and accessed NetWare resources via a Novell client specifically designed for that client.

QUESTION 36

What kind of access category does NetWare 6.5 use to provide clients with direct access to NSS using the clients' native file access protocols?

A. Native file access

B. Traditional client access

C. Browser-based access

D. NetWare access

EXPLANATION

Using native file access protocols means that users can browse folders and directories just as if they were connected to a server that runs the same file access protocols by default.

4

QUESTION 37

What is the name of the software that, when installed on Windows clients, allows them to access directories on a NetWare 6.5 server?

A. NetModule

B. NetClient

C. NetFiles

D. NetDrive

EXPLANATION

Rather than using the Windows native filesystem access protocol, CIFS, NetDrive uses Internet protocols, such as HTTP and FTP.

QUESTION 38

What access category is the simplest way for users to access a NetWare 6.5 server?

A. Native file access

B. Browser-based access

C. Traditional client access

D. NetWare access

EXPLANATION

Perhaps the simplest way for users to access NetWare 6.5 files and directories is through a Web browser.

QUESTION 39

What does a client need to use Novell's NetStorage tool?

- **A.** TCP/IP
- **B.** IPX/SPX
- **C.** Windows XP
- **D.** Linux

EXPLANATION

To use NetStorage, clients need only have the TCP/IP protocols installed and configured.

QUESTION 40

What is the name of the Novell's tool for integrating eDirectory and Windows Active Directory or Windows NT domain data?

- **A.** NetDir
- **B.** DirXML
- **C.** NetXML
- **D.** e-Dir

EXPLANATION

With DirXML installed and configured on both the NetWare and Windows servers in an organization, the servers can share directory data.

QUESTION 41

What is true about DirXML? (Choose 2)

- **A.** With DirXML, an eDirectory is the only information source
- **B.** With DirXML, an Active Directory is the only information source
- **C.** With DirXML, an eDirectory can be the information source
- **D.** With DirXML, an Active Directory can be the information source

EXPLANATION

A network administrator can configure DirXML so that either Active Directory or eDirectory is the authoritative source for directory information.

QUESTION 42

What is the name of Novell's tools designed to simplify NetWare access for users running the Linux NOS?

A. Nterprise Linux Services
B. DirXML for Linux
C. NetXML for Linux
D. e-Directory Linux Services

EXPLANATION

Nterprise Linux Services consists of client tools for accessing eDirectory, development tools for integrating Linux servers with DirXML, plus browser-based file and print services.

QUESTION 43

What is true about HTTP servers?

A. They might not be visible to the Internet
B. They are always visible to the Internet
C. They can only be visible to the Internet
D. They can only be visible within a private network

EXPLANATION

An HTTP server does not even have to be connected to the Internet.

QUESTION 44

A private network that offers HTTP access to documents, file sharing, e-mail, and collaboration services within an enterprise is known as:

A. Extranet
B. Intranet
C. Internet
D. Privatenet

EXPLANATION

A network or part of a network that uses browser-based services to exchange information within an enterprise is known as an intranet.

QUESTION 45

What is one of the most important characteristics of an intranet?
- **A.** It is browser based
- **B.** Security
- **C.** It cannot extend across an organization's WAN
- **D.** It must run over a private WAN

EXPLANATION

An intranet is defined by its security policies—that is, by the fact that it allows access only to authorized users who belong to a certain organization.

QUESTION 46

A network that uses Internet-like services and protocols to exchange information within an organization *and* with certain authorized users outside of that organization is known as:
- **A.** Internet
- **B.** Intranet
- **C.** Extranet
- **D.** Ethernet

EXPLANATION

A construction company might use an extranet, for example, to allow its employees to access company documents from home or from a job site and also to allow contractors to submit bids for jobs.

QUESTION 47

What can be used to quickly and easily verify that a node's NIC is transmitting and receiving signals properly?
- **A.** Router
- **B.** Switch
- **C.** Hub
- **D.** Crossover cable

EXPLANATION

In a crossover cable, the transmit and receive wire pairs in one of the connectors are reversed. This reversal enables you to use a crossover cable to directly interconnect two nodes without using an intervening connectivity device.

QUESTION 48

What is the name for a network signal generator device?

- **A.** Tone locator
- **B.** Signal generator
- **C.** Tone generator
- **D.** Tone source

EXPLANATION

A tone generator is a small electronic device that issues a signal on a wire pair.

QUESTION 49

What is the name for a network signal detector device?

- **A.** Tone locator
- **B.** Tone generator
- **C.** Signal locator
- **D.** Signal receptor

EXPLANATION

A tone locator is a device that emits a tone when it detects electrical activity on a wire pair.

QUESTION 50

The combination of a tone generator and locator devices is known as:

- **A.** Eagle and mouse
- **B.** Fox and hound
- **C.** Tone box
- **D.** Toner

EXPLANATION

The tone locator (the hound) chases the tone generator (the fox).

QUESTION 51

What other characteristics about a cable can be tested using tone generator and locator devices?

    A. Defects on the cable

    B. Length does not exceed IEEE standards

    C. Length does not exceed IETF standards

    D. None of the above

EXPLANATION

Tone generator and locator are used only to determine where a wire pair terminates.

QUESTION 52

What other network components can be tested using a tone generator?

    A. A workstation's NIC

    B. A switch port

    C. A router port

    D. None of the above

EXPLANATION

A tone generator should never be used on a wire that's connected to a device's port or network adapter. Because a tone generator transmits electricity over the wire, it may damage the device or network adapter.

QUESTION 53

What is the name of the instrument used to measure voltage on a wire?

    A. Multimeter

    B. Ohmmeter

    C. Voltmeter

    D. Millimeter

EXPLANATION

Voltmeter is the instrument that measures the pressure of an electric current.

QUESTION 54

What is the name of the instrument used to measure resistance on a wire?
- **A.** Multimeter
- **B.** Ohmmeter
- **C.** Voltmeter
- **D.** Millimeter

EXPLANATION

Resistance is measured in ohms.

4

QUESTION 55

What is the name of a simple instrument that can measure many characteristics of an electric circuit, including its resistance and voltage?
- **A.** Multimeter
- **B.** Ohmmeter
- **C.** Voltmeter
- **D.** Millimeter

EXPLANATION

Although a person could use separate instruments for measuring impedance, resistance, and voltage on a wire, it is more convenient to have one instrument that accomplishes all of these functions. The multimeter is such an instrument.

QUESTION 56

What electrical characteristic can tell you where faults in a cable lie?
- **A.** Voltage
- **B.** Impedance
- **C.** Resistant
- **D.** All of the above

EXPLANATION

A certain amount of impedance is required for a signal to be properly transmitted and interpreted. However, very high or low levels of impedance can signify a damaged wire, incorrect pairing, or a termination point.

QUESTION 57

What electrical characteristic cannot be measured by a multimeter?

A. Voltage
B. Resistance
C. Noise
D. None of the above

EXPLANATION

Multimeters vary in their degree of sophistication and features. Some merely show voltage levels, for example, while others can measure the level of noise on a circuit at any moment with extreme precision.

QUESTION 58

What tools are useful when troubleshooting a Physical layer problem? (Choose 2)

A. Cable checker
B. Continuity tester
C. Continuity checker
D. Cable continuity

EXPLANATION

Tools used for testing the continuity of the cable may be called cable checkers or continuity testers.

QUESTION 59

How many parts does a continuity tester for copper-based wires have?

A. 1
B. 2
C. 3
D. 4

EXPLANATION

A continuity tester consists of the base unit that generates the voltage and the remote unit that detects the voltage.

QUESTION 60

What other types of tests can a continuity tester perform? (Choose 2)
- **A.** Cables are documented
- **B.** Cables are color-coded
- **C.** Crossed wires
- **D.** Exposed wires

EXPLANATION

In addition to checking cable continuity, some continuity testers will verify that the wires in a UTP or STP cable are paired correctly and that they are not shorted, exposed, or crossed.

4

QUESTION 61

What is true about continuity testers?
- **A.** They can only be used with copper-based wires
- **B.** They can only test UTP cables
- **C.** They can test other types of cabling besides copper-based wires
- **D.** They can only test STP cables

EXPLANATION

Continuity testers for fiber-optic networks also exist.

QUESTION 62

What is a good practice when cabling your network?
- **A.** Test your cables only if you make them
- **B.** Test your cables only if you buy them
- **C.** Never test your cables
- **D.** Always test your cables

EXPLANATION

Whether you make your own cables or purchase cabling from a reputable vendor, test the cable to ensure that it meets your network's required standards.

QUESTION 63

When using a continuity tester you should:

    A. Never test a live cable

    B. Test only live cables

    C. Shut down the server

    D. Shut down the router

EXPLANATION

You should always disconnect the cable from the network and then test its continuity.

QUESTION 64

From the following list, which one is a popular manufacturer of continuity testers?

    A. Fluke

    B. Sistei

    C. Soni

    D. None of the above

EXPLANATION

Popular manufacturers of these cable testing devices include Belkin, Fluke, Microtest, and Paladin.

QUESTION 65

From the following list, what statement is correct?

    A. Both cable performance tester and continuity tester are equivalent

    B. A continuity tester is more powerful than a cable performance tester

    C. A cable performance tester is more powerful than a continuity tester

    D. There is no such device as a cable performance tester

EXPLANATION

If you need to know more than whether a cable is simply carrying current, you can use a cable performance tester.

QUESTION 66

What tool can be used to measure the way a signal reflects?
   A. Multimeter
   B. Cable checker
   C. Continuity tester
   D. Time domain reflectometer

EXPLANATION

A TDR issues a signal on a cable and then measures the way the signal bounces back (or reflects) to the TDR.

4

QUESTION 67

On what kind of network can a cable performance tester be used?
   A. STP networks
   B. Coaxial networks
   C. Fiber–optic network
   D. All of the above

EXPLANATION

In addition to performance testers for coaxial and twisted-pair networks, you can also find performance testers for fiber-optic networks.

QUESTION 68

What does OTDR stand for?
   A. Original time domain reflectometer
   B. Optical time domain reflectometer
   C. Object Template for Directory Resources
   D. Optical time division reflector

EXPLANATION

Cable performance testers for fiber-optic networks use OTDRs instead of the conventional TDRs.

QUESTION 69

What signal characteristic can be measured by an OTDR?

    A. EMP interference

    B. Attenuation

    C. EMP generation

    D. None of the above

EXPLANATION

An OTDR can accurately measure the length of the fiber, determine the location of faulty splices, breaks, connectors, or bends, and measure attenuation over the cable.

QUESTION 70

Which statement is true from the following list?

    A. A cable performance tester is more sophisticated than a continuity tester

    B. A continuity tester is more expensive than a cable performance tester

    C. A multimeter is more sophisticated than a performance tester

    D. A cable checker is more expensive than a performance tester

EXPLANATION

Because of their sophistication, performance testers for both copper and fiber-optic cables cost significantly more than continuity testers.

QUESTION 71

Which property protects network components from being altered or modified by unauthorized means?

    A. Integrity

    B. Confidentiality

    C. Availability

    D. Privacy

EXPLANATION

Integrity refers to the soundness of a network's programs, data, services, devices, and connections.

QUESTION 72

Which property specifies that users should always have access to authorized network resources?

    A. Integrity

    B. Confidentiality

    C. Privacy

    D. Availability

EXPLANATION

Availability of a file or system refers to how consistently and reliably it can be accessed by authorized personnel.

4

QUESTION 73

What can help you to increase the availability of your network resources?

    A. An insurance policy

    B. Keeping a copy of your data in a safe place

    C. Relaxed security policies

    D. No security at all

EXPLANATION

To ensure high availability, you need a well-planned and well-configured network, as well as data backups, redundant devices, and protection from malicious intruders who could potentially immobilize the network.

QUESTION 74

From the following list, what can compromise the integrity of your network?

    A. Using a good antivirus application

    B. Having your firewall well configured

    C. Relaxed security policies

    D. Having updated data backups

EXPLANATION

A number of phenomena may compromise both integrity and availability, including security breaches, natural disasters (such as tornadoes, floods, hurricanes, and ice storms), malicious intruders, power flaws, and human error.

QUESTION 75

From the following list, what can compromise the availability of your network?

A. Having Uninterruptible Power Suppliers attached to critical networks components

B. Running an NOS without the latest updates and patches

C. A light rain

D. Good room temperature control systems

EXPLANATION

A number of phenomena may compromise both integrity and availability, including security breaches, natural disasters (such as tornadoes, floods, hurricanes, and ice storms), malicious intruders, power flaws, and human error.

QUESTION 76

What is a good practice for protecting your network?

A. Allow only network administrators to create or modify NOS and application system files

B. Allow any user to modify your network

C. Allow any user to change network components configurations

D. Allow users to modify their own workstations' TCP/IP settings

EXPLANATION

If you have ever supported computer users, you know that they sometimes unintentionally harm data, applications, software configurations, or even hardware.

QUESTION 77

What should you do for protecting your network?

A. Trigger alarms every time a user modifies a file

B. Trigger alarms when a user accesses a network resource

C. Let users install new network monitoring devices

D. Monitor your network for unauthorized access or changes

EXPLANATION

You can install programs that routinely check whether and when the files you've specified (for example, server.exe on a NetWare server) have changed.

QUESTION 78

Although you should monitor your network for unauthorized changes, what should you do about authorized changes?

A. Trigger a silent alarm
B. Trigger an audio alarm
C. Log them
D. Do nothing

EXPLANATION

You have learned about the importance of change management when troubleshooting networks. Routine changes should also be documented in a change management system.

4

QUESTION 79

An implementation in which more than one component is installed and ready to use for storing, processing, or transporting data is also referred to as:

A. Integrity
B. Redundancy
C. Privacy
D. Confidentiality

EXPLANATION

Redundancy is intended to eliminate single points of failure.

QUESTION 80

What property is a factor in maintaining high network availability?

A. Atomic processes
B. Privacy
C. Confidentiality
D. Redundancy

EXPLANATION

Redundancy is intended to eliminate single points of failure.

QUESTION 81

As a good network manager, what is a good habit you should have for protecting your network?

A. Perform regular health checks on the network

B. Install antivirus software only on critical servers

C. Keep default administrator account passwords so your staff does not need to remember new complex passwords

D. Do not waste your time checking system logs

EXPLANATION

Prevention is the best weapon against network downtime.

QUESTION 82

What will help you prevent network failures? (Choose 2)

A. Do not share your knowledge of the network

B. Install antivirus software only on critical servers

C. Establish a baseline

D. Regular network monitoring

EXPLANATION

For example, if your network monitor alerts you to rapidly rising utilization on a critical network segment, you can analyze the network to discover where the problem lies and perhaps fix it before it takes down the segment.

QUESTION 83

What is a good way of detecting errors in their early stages? (Choose 2)

A. Using strong passwords

B. Log error messages

C. Check system logs

D. Upgrading your hardware at the first symptom of bad performance

EXPLANATION

By keeping track of system errors and trends in performance, you have a better chance of correcting problems before they cause a hard disk failure and potentially damage your system files.

QUESTION 84

Where does a Linux server keep logs from system services by default?

A. /var_log

B. Var/Log

C. /Var/log

D. /var/log

EXPLANATION

On a Linux server, a file called messages located in the /var/log directory collects error messages from system services such as DNS.

4

QUESTION 85

How can you help your network environment recover faster from a disaster?

A. Keep backups, boot disks, and emergency repair disks current and available

B. Keep your insurance policy in a safe place

C. Use strong passwords with your administrator account

D. Log all error messages

EXPLANATION

If your filesystem or critical boot files become corrupted by a system crash, you can use the emergency or boot disks to recover the system.

QUESTION 86

What is a key factor in protecting your network?

A. Allowing users to download applications from the Internet

B. Allowing users to install applications

C. Policies

D. All of the above

EXPLANATION

Everyone in your organization should know what he is allowed to do on the network.

QUESTION 87

What will help you to act correctly in case of a natural disaster?

A. Security policies
B. Disaster recovery policies
C. A good firewall
D. Well-configured routers

EXPLANATION

Key personnel in your organization should be familiar with your disaster recovery plan, which should detail your strategy for restoring network functionality in case of an unexpected failure.

QUESTION 88

Network policies can directly affect your network: (Choose 2)

A. Integrity
B. Domain
C. Availability
D. ISP

EXPLANATION

These measures are merely first steps to ensuring network integrity and availability, but they are essential.

QUESTION 89

What is an advantage of recording system changes?

A. It eliminates network delays
B. It gives you network redundancy
C. It allows you to create good information filters
D. It lets you know more about your network

EXPLANATION

Recording system changes enables you and your colleagues to understand what's happening to your network and protect it from harm.

QUESTION 90

What will help you troubleshoot a network problem?
- **A.** Redundancy
- **B.** Recording changes
- **C.** Disaster recovery plan
- **D.** Security policy

EXPLANATION

Before taking troubleshooting steps that may create more problems and further reduce the availability of the system, you could review the change management log.

4

QUESTION 91

What is the name for a program that replicates itself with the intent to infect more computers, either through network connections or through the exchange of external storage devices?
- **A.** Trojan mail
- **B.** Trojan horses
- **C.** Virus
- **D.** Worm horses

EXPLANATION

Viruses are typically copied to a computer's storage device without the user's knowledge.

QUESTION 92

What is true about viruses?
- **A.** They might not cause any damage to your computer
- **B.** They always damage your systems
- **C.** They are always immediately identified
- **D.** They always delete your files

EXPLANATION

Some viruses cause no harm and can remain unnoticed on a system indefinitely.

QUESTION 93

What is the name for a program that disguises itself as something useful but actually harms your system?

A. Virus
B. Trojan horse
C. Worm
D. Logic bomb

EXPLANATION

The first Trojan horse was the famous wooden horse in which soldiers were hidden.

QUESTION 94

What is the correct statement?

A. Viruses only infect Windows-based workstations
B. Viruses only infect servers
C. Viruses cannot infect servers
D. Viruses can infect a Linux-based system

EXPLANATION

Viruses can infect computers running any type of operating system.

QUESTION 95

What type of virus positions its code in the boot sector of a computer's hard disk so that when the computer boots up, the virus runs in place of the computer's normal system files?

A. Macro
B. File-infected
C. Boot sector
D. Worms

EXPLANATION

A way of protecting a computer against boot sector viruses is preventing it from booting from an external disk such as a floppy disk.

QUESTION 96

What can be said about boot sector viruses?

  A. They are the most destructive type of viruses
  B. They cause no harm
  C. Some of them are destructive
  D. They never delete files on your system

EXPLANATION

Boot sector viruses vary in their destructiveness.

QUESTION 97

What is the first step for removing a boot sector virus?

  A. Boot up from a clean write-protected disk
  B. Boot up from the hard disk
  C. Disable write privileges on your hard disk
  D. Boot up from a clean write-enabled disk

EXPLANATION

Only after the computer is booted from a source other than the infected hard disk can you run software to remove the boot sector virus.

QUESTION 98

What type of viruses takes the form of a macro (such as the kind used in a word processing or spreadsheet program), which may be executed as the user works with a program?

  A. Worm
  B. Macro
  C. Boot sector
  D. Hoax

EXPLANATION

A macro virus can be transmitted on a WordPerfect document as an attachment to an e-mail message.

QUESTION 99

What was the first type of viruses to infect data files rather than executable files?

   A. Boot sector
   B. Logic bomb
   C. Macro
   D. Worm

EXPLANATION

If a document contains a macro virus, when the recipient opens the document, the macro runs, and all future documents created or saved by that program are infected.

QUESTION 100

What is a characteristic of macro viruses?

   A. They do not spread quickly
   B. They are very complex
   C. They spread on executable files
   D. They are easy to create

EXPLANATION

Macro viruses are quick to emerge and spread because they are easy to write, and because users share data files more frequently than executable files.

QUESTION 101

How does a file-infected virus spread?

   A. Through data files
   B. Through macro files
   C. Through executable files
   D. Through Word documents

EXPLANATION

When an infected executable file runs, the virus copies itself to memory. Later, the virus attaches itself to other executable files.

QUESTION 102

Why can file-infected viruses be very devastating?
- **A.** They are transmitted on data files
- **B.** They stay in memory
- **C.** They run as macros
- **D.** They are easy to create

EXPLANATION

File-infected viruses stay in memory while you continue to work on your computer, infecting numerous programs and requiring that you disinfect your computer, as well as reinstall virtually all software.

QUESTION 103

What is a symptom of a file-infected virus infection?
- **A.** Bigger file sizes
- **B.** Modified Word documents
- **C.** Modified music files
- **D.** Infected boot sector

EXPLANATION

Symptoms of virus infection may include damaged program files, inexplicable file size increases, changed icons for programs, strange messages that appear when you attempt to run a program, or the inability to run a program.

QUESTION 104

What is true about file-infected viruses?
- **A.** They always have devastating effects
- **B.** They all are harmless viruses
- **C.** Some of them are harmless viruses
- **D.** They infect data files

EXPLANATION

"Harmony.A" is an example of a file-infected virus. It only increases the size of and adds a message to all executable files on a hard disk installed with a Windows operating system.

QUESTION 105

Worms are technically misidentified as:

  A. File-infected virus
  B. Boot sector virus
  C. Logic bomb
  D. Virus

EXPLANATION

Worms are programs that run independently and travel between computers and across networks.

QUESTION 106

How can a worm spread?

  A. Through an e-mail message
  B. Through an e-mail attachment
  C. Through an infected boot sector
  D. All of the above

EXPLANATION

Macro viruses may be transmitted by any type of file transfer.

QUESTION 107

What is a difference between worms and viruses?

  A. Worms cannot carry viruses
  B. Worms modify files
  C. Viruses modify files
  D. Viruses carry worms

EXPLANATION

Worms do not alter other programs in the same way that viruses do, but they may carry viruses.

QUESTION 108

Trojan horses are technically misidentified as:
- **A.** Viruses
- **B.** Worms
- **C.** Hoax viruses
- **D.** Macro viruses

EXPLANATION

A Trojan horse (or Trojan) is a program that claims to do something useful but instead harms the computer or system.

QUESTION 109

How can you clean a computer infected by a known Trojan?
- **A.** Manually delete the original infected file
- **B.** Manually delete all infected files
- **C.** Delete all infected data files
- **D.** Use antivirus software

EXPLANATION

Virus detection programs recognize known Trojan horses and eradicate them.

QUESTION 110

How can you prevent a Trojan infection on your computer?
- **A.** Download applications from the Internet
- **B.** Download drivers from generic support sites
- **C.** Only execute applications that you have downloaded from known sources
- **D.** Open e-mail attachments warning you about a new Trojan horse

EXPLANATION

The best way to guard against Trojan horses is to refrain from downloading an executable file whose origins you can't confirm.

QUESTION 111

What is the name for the capacity for a system to continue performing despite an unexpected hardware or software malfunction?

A. Integrity
B. Fault tolerance
C. Confidentiality
D. Security

EXPLANATION

Another key factor in maintaining the availability and integrity of data is fault tolerance.

QUESTION 112

What is the name for a deviation from a specified level of system performance for a given period of time?

A. Failure
B. Fault
C. Tolerance
D. Consistency

EXPLANATION

A failure occurs when something doesn't work as promised or as planned.

QUESTION 113

What term involves the malfunction of one component of a system?

A. Resistance
B. Failure
C. Fault
D. Integrity

EXPLANATION

A fault can result in a failure.

QUESTION 114

What is the goal of a fault-tolerant system?

A. Protect your firewall
B. Clean virus-infected files
C. Prevent failures from progressing to faults
D. Prevent faults from progressing to failures

EXPLANATION

At the highest level of fault tolerance, a system remains unaffected by even the most drastic problem, such as a regional power outage.

4

QUESTION 115

What network aspect should you also consider when developing a fault-tolerant network?

A. Insurance policies
B. Physical environment
C. Your staff technical skills
D. All of the above

EXPLANATION

Part of your data protection plan involves protecting your network from excessive heat or moisture, break-ins, and natural disasters.

QUESTION 116

What kind of failures should be considered when implementing a fault-tolerant network?

A. Air supply failure
B. Water supply failure
C. Power failure
D. Water supply fluctuations

EXPLANATION

No matter where you live, you have probably experienced a complete loss of power (a blackout) or a temporary dimming of lights (a brownout).

QUESTION 117

What is the name for a momentary increase in voltage due to lightning strikes, solar flares, or electrical problems?

A. Surge
B. Noise
C. Brownout
D. Blackout

EXPLANATION

Surges may last only a few thousandths of a second, but they can degrade a computer's power supply. Surges are common.

QUESTION 118

What is the name for a fluctuation in voltage levels caused by other devices on the network or electromagnetic interference?

A. Surge
B. Blackout
C. Brownout
D. Noise

EXPLANATION

Some noise is unavoidable on an electrical circuit, but excessive noise may cause a power supply to malfunction.

QUESTION 119

What is the name for a momentary decrease in voltage, also known as a *sag*?

A. Surge
B. Blackout
C. Brownout
D. Noise

EXPLANATION

An overtaxed electrical system may cause brownouts, which you may recognize in your home as a dimming of the lights.

QUESTION 120

What is the name for a complete power loss?
- **A.** Surge
- **B.** Blackout
- **C.** Brownout
- **D.** Noise

EXPLANATION

Unlike brownouts, blackouts may last indefinitely, leaving your devices powerless.

4

QUESTION 121

What is a popular way of ensuring your devices will not be affected by a blackout?
- **A.** Surge protector
- **B.** UPS
- **C.** Noise reducer
- **D.** Noise protector

EXPLANATION

A UPS is a battery-operated power source directly attached to one or more devices.

QUESTION 122

How many UPS categories exist?
- **A.** 2
- **B.** 3
- **C.** 4
- **D.** 5

EXPLANATION

UPSs are classified into standby and online.

QUESTION 123

What type of UPS detects when there is a power loss and starts feeding devices from its own battery for the duration of the power failure?

   A. Smart
   B. Inline
   C. Online
   D. Standby

EXPLANATION

Standby UPS provides continuous voltage to a device by switching virtually instantaneously to the battery when it detects a loss of power from the wall outlet.

QUESTION 124

What is a common problem with standby UPSs?

   A. They can only operate for 10 minutes
   B. They have high battery consumption rates
   C. Technically, they do not provide continuous voltage to a device
   D. Their battery power lasts only for one hour

EXPLANATION

One problem exists with standby UPSs: In the brief amount of time that it takes the UPS to discover that power from the wall outlet has faltered, a device may have already detected the power loss and shut down or restarted.

QUESTION 125

What kind of UPS feeds devices from its own battery even if there is no power failure?

   A. Standby
   B. Online
   C. Offline
   D. Inline

EXPLANATION

An online UPS uses the A/C power from the wall outlet to continuously charge its battery, while providing power to a network device through its battery.

QUESTION 126

What is a factor to consider when choosing a UPS for your devices?

    A. Amount of power needed by your device

    B. Security features

    C. Case color

    D. All of the above

EXPLANATION

The more power required by your device, the more powerful must be the UPS.

4

QUESTION 127

How many volt-amps (VAs) are approximately equivalent to 1 watt (W)?

    A. 0.4

    B. 0.9

    C. 1.1

    D. 1.4

EXPLANATION

A desktop computer, for example, may use a 200 W power supply and therefore require a UPS capable of at least 280 VA to keep the CPU running in case of a blackout.

QUESTION 128

What should you consider when choosing a UPS?

    A. Current equipment only

    B. Only printer servers

    C. Both current and future equipment

    D. Only servers

EXPLANATION

Determining your power needs can be a challenge. You must account for your existing equipment and consider how you might upgrade the supported device(s) over the next several years.

QUESTION 129

Knowing that a medium-size server that relies on a 574 VA UPS to remain functional for 20 minutes, what is correct?

A. It will require a less powerful UPS to remain functional for 90 minutes

B. It will require a more powerful UPS to remain functional for 90 minutes

C. It will require a more powerful UPS to remain functional for 15 minutes

D. It can use the same UPS to remain functional for 100 minutes

EXPLANATION

The longer you anticipate needing a UPS to power your device, the more powerful your UPS must be.

QUESTION 130

What other kinds of power failure should a UPS control? (Choose 2)

A. Surge

B. EMI

C. EMP

D. Noise

EXPLANATION

A UPS should also offer surge suppression to protect against surges and line conditioning, or filtering, to guard against line noise.

QUESTION 131

In what unit is noise expressed?

A. amp (A)

B. volt (V)

C. watt (W)

D. decibel (dB)

EXPLANATION

The higher the decibel level, the greater the protection offered by a noise filtering system.

QUESTION 132

What is true about UPS prices?

  A. Prices vary, depending of the NOS used with the protected server
  B. A UNIX server can use a cheaper UPS
  C. Cost depends on the unit's size
  D. Windows-based devices can only use very expensive UPSs

EXPLANATION

Prices for good UPSs vary widely, depending on the unit's size and extra features.

4

QUESTION 133

What can be used to power an electrical generator?

  A. Liquid oxygen
  B. Liquid nitrogen
  C. Gun powder
  D. None of the above

EXPLANATION

Generators can be powered by diesel, liquid propane gas, natural gas, or steam.

QUESTION 134

What is true about electrical generators?

  A. They offer surge protection
  B. They offer noiseless electricity
  C. They provide electricity full of noise
  D. They are always combined with a UPS to provide noiseless electricity

EXPLANATION

They do not provide surge protection, but they do provide electricity that's free from noise.

QUESTION 135

For what reason are generators usually combined with UPSs?

A. So the UPS can provide electricity while the generator starts up

B. So the generator can provide electricity while the UPS starts up

C. To eliminate noise from the electricity provided by the generator

D. To reduce costs

EXPLANATION

Generators are typically combined with large UPSs to ensure that clean power is always available.

QUESTION 136

What aspects should you consider when choosing a generator? (Choose 2)

A. The number of rooms in your building

B. Power demand

C. Running time

D. All of the above

EXPLANATION

When choosing a generator, you should calculate your organization's crucial electrical demands to determine the generator's optimal size. Also estimate how long the generator may be required to power your building.

QUESTION 137

What is the key factor when designing a fault-tolerant network?

A. Retransmit data as soon as a failure is detected

B. Do not allow data to be rerouted in case of a failure

C. Create a fixed path for data to travel and protect that path

D. That data can reach its destination in more than one way

EXPLANATION

The key to fault tolerance in network design is supplying multiple paths data can use to travel from any one point to another.

QUESTION 138

What WAN topology offers the best fault tolerance?
  A. Partial mesh
  B. Half mesh
  C. Full mesh
  D. Star with a parallel backbone

EXPLANATION

A partial mesh topology offers some redundancy but is not as fault tolerant as a full mesh WAN, because it offers fewer alternate routes for data.

4

QUESTION 139

What other technology can help you construct a highly fault-tolerant network?
  A. SONET
  B. Bluetooth
  C. Single ring
  D. Bus

EXPLANATION

SONET technology relies on a dual fiber-optic ring for transmission.

QUESTION 140

What should you do to provide a highly available connection to the Internet?
  A. Use a full mesh topology
  B. Establish redundant links to the Internet
  C. Implement a SONET ring
  D. Use a partial mesh network

EXPLANATION

Mesh topologies and SONET rings are good choices for highly available enterprise networks. But what about connections to the Internet or data backup connections? You may need to establish more than one of these links.

QUESTION 141

What is the main disadvantage of redundancy?

A. Time

B. Cost

C. Security

D. Availability

EXPLANATION

If you subscribed to two different service providers, for two T1 links for example, you would probably double your monthly leasing costs.

QUESTION 142

What is the name of the property when a particular component immediately assumes the duties of an identical component?

A. Fail-back

B. Roll-over

C. Fail-over

D. Roll-back

EXPLANATION

Even if one router's NIC fails, for example, fail-over ensures that the router's other NIC can automatically handle the first server's responsibilities.

QUESTION 143

If you can't provide fail-over capable components, what should you use instead?

A. Insured components

B. Cold parts

C. Plug-in parts

D. Hot-swappable parts

EXPLANATION

The term "hot-swappable" refers to identical components that can be changed (or swapped) while a machine is still running (hot).

QUESTION 144

Select the correct statement from the following list:
   A. A fail-over capable component will not solve all connection problems
   B. A hot-swappable switch will address all network faults
   C. You will not suffer from network faults if you use a fail-over capable router
   D. You will not suffer from network faults if you use a hot-swappable router

EXPLANATION

Purchasing connectivity devices with hot-swappable or fail-over capable components does not address all faults that may occur in a connection.

QUESTION 145

Automatic distribution of traffic over multiple links or processors to optimize response is also known as:
   A. Re-balance
   B. Even traffic
   C. Load balancing
   D. Tuning traffic

EXPLANATION

Load balancing would maximize the throughput between two points, because the aggregate traffic flowing between the two points could move over either T1 link (assuming a redundant T1 link between the end points), avoiding potential bottlenecks on a single T1 connection.

QUESTION 146

What is a less expensive redundancy option?
   A. Dial-back WAN link
   B. Backup links
   C. WAN links
   D. Split WAN link

EXPLANATION

For example, a company that depends on a Frame Relay WAN might also have an access server with a DSL or dial-up link that automatically contacts the remote site when it detects a failure of the primary link.

QUESTION 147

What is a true statement about redundancy?

    A. Redundancy is only valid for connectivity devices

    B. Redundancy can also be applied to computers

    C. Redundancy only improves fault tolerance on routers

    D. Redundancy only improves fault tolerance on switches

EXPLANATION

As with other devices, you can make servers more fault-tolerant by supplying them with redundant components.

QUESTION 148

What are common redundant parts on a network server? (Choose 2)

    A. Network adapter

    B. Display

    C. Storage units

    D. Keyboard

EXPLANATION

Critical servers often contain redundant NICs, processors, and hard disks.

QUESTION 149

What is correct about load balancing?

    A. It is a redundancy disadvantage

    B. Technically, it is the same as fault-tolerance

    C. It is part of a fault-tolerant design

    D. It helps in justifying redundant components

EXPLANATION

Although load balancing does not technically fall under the category of fault tolerance, it helps justify the purchase of redundant components that do contribute to fault tolerance.

QUESTION 150

What is the name of a fault-tolerance technique in which one device or component duplicates the activities of another?

    A. Copy
    B. Mirroring
    C. Reflection
    D. Imaging

EXPLANATION

In server mirroring, one server continually duplicates the transactions and data storage of another.

QUESTION 151

What is the name of the term that refers to the dynamic copying of data from one location to another?

    A. Reflection
    B. Mirroring
    C. Replication
    D. Imaging

EXPLANATION

Server mirroring is considered to be a form of replication.

QUESTION 152

What is one disadvantage of server mirroring?

    A. Diminished network performance
    B. Either server can be "up" at any time
    C. Servers must be in different locations
    D. Servers must be in the same location

EXPLANATION

It takes time for the twin server to digest everything the other server does and repeat it.

QUESTION 153

What is the name for the fault-tolerance technique that links multiple servers together to act as a single server?

A. Replication
B. Mirroring
C. Clustering
D. Time sharing

EXPLANATION

In this configuration, clustered servers share processing duties and appear as a single server to users.

QUESTION 154

What fault-tolerance technique is more cost effective than mirroring for large networks?

A. Client mirroring
B. Clustering
C. Replication
D. Database replication

EXPLANATION

If one server in the cluster fails, the other servers in the cluster automatically take over its data transaction and storage responsibilities.

QUESTION 155

What is one difference of clustering regarding server mirroring?

A. In clustering, all servers must be identical
B. With mirroring, servers must be in the same exact location
C. With clustering, servers must be in different locations
D. Unlike with mirroring, users will not notice a server switch

EXPLANATION

With clustering, the fail-over and recovery processes are transparent to network users.

QUESTION 156

What is one disadvantage of clustering?

- **A.** Servers must be geographically close
- **B.** Users will notice a server switch
- **C.** Server switching is a manual process
- **D.** Server switching always takes more than 5 minutes

EXPLANATION

Typically, clustering is implemented among servers located in the same data room.

QUESTION 157

What is one advantage of clustering over server mirroring?

- **A.** Servers do not perform other functions except when taking over a failed server
- **B.** A server can perform its own data processing
- **C.** Servers must be in different locations
- **D.** It is a hardware-based solution

EXPLANATION

Not only does this ability to perform multiple functions reduce the cost of ownership for a cluster of servers, but it also improves performance.

QUESTION 158

What is true about clustering?

- **A.** It is implemented through a combination of software and hardware
- **B.** It is a hardware-based solution
- **C.** It is a software-based solution
- **D.** Microsoft does not offer support for clustering

EXPLANATION

Novell NetWare 5.x and 6.x and Microsoft Windows Server 2003 incorporate options for server clustering.

QUESTION 159

What is the correct statement?

A. There are no fault tolerance techniques for data storage

B. You should not worry about data storage availability

C. You should also consider data storage availability

D. Data storage servers will never experience a failure

EXPLANATION

Related to the availability and fault tolerance of servers is the availability and fault tolerance of data storage.

QUESTION 160

What is the name for a collection of disks that provides fault tolerance for shared data and applications?

A. RCA

B. ROAM

C. RAS

D. RAID

EXPLANATION

RAID stands for Redundant Array of Independent (or Inexpensive) Disks.

QUESTION 161

For a system using RAID, how do the multiple disks in a RAID drive appear?

A. As a single drive

B. As multiple drives

C. As two drives

D. As three drives

EXPLANATION

A group of hard disks is called a disk array (or a drive).

QUESTION 162

What is one advantage of using RAID?

 A. Provides data privacy
 B. Offers data confidentiality
 C. Improves data availability
 D. Has a better data encryption mechanism

EXPLANATION

One advantage of using RAID is that a single disk failure will not cause a catastrophic loss of data.

4

QUESTION 163

What is true about RAID?

 A. It is always a hardware-based solution
 B. It can also be a software solution
 C. It is always a software-based solution
 D. Hardware RAID is less expensive than software RAID

EXPLANATION

RAID may be implemented as a hardware or software solution.

QUESTION 164

What are the components of hardware RAID?

 A. A set of disks and a disk controller
 B. A set of disks only
 C. A disk controller only
 D. None of the above

EXPLANATION

The hardware RAID array is managed exclusively by the RAID disk controller.

QUESTION 165

What is true about software RAID?

    A. It also requires a special disk controller

    B. It is more expensive than hardware RAID

    C. It always has better performance than hardware RAID

    D. Its performance has improved in the last few years

EXPLANATION

With today's fast processors, software RAID performance rivals that of hardware RAID, which was formerly regarded as faster.

QUESTION 166

What is a main disadvantage of RAID level 0?

    A. It does not use multiple partitions effectively

    B. It is not a fault-tolerant method

    C. It has the worst performance

    D. It is not easy to implement

EXPLANATION

RAID level 0 does not provide true redundancy.

QUESTION 167

What technique does RAID level 1 use to implement redundancy?

    A. Disk stripping

    B. Disk stripping with parity ECC

    C. Disk mirroring

    D. Disk roaming

EXPLANATION

RAID level 1 is also known as disk mirroring.

QUESTION 168

What is one advantage of disk mirroring?

A. Dynamic data backup

B. It is a inexpensive solution

C. It does not require resynchronization after a disk failure

D. It is the most effective way of protecting data

EXPLANATION

If one disk in the array fails, the disk array controller automatically switches to the disk that was mirroring the failed disk.

QUESTION 169

What is the name for a technique in which data is continually copied from one disk to another when it is saved and a separate disk controller is used for each different disk?

A. Disk mirroring

B. Disk duplication

C. Disk replication

D. Disk duplexing

EXPLANATION

Disk duplexing provides added fault tolerance because a disk controller failure will not render data inaccessible.

QUESTION 170

What term refers to the mechanism used to verify the integrity of data by making the number of bits in a byte sum to either an odd or even number?

A. RAID level 3

B. ECE

C. Hash value

D. Parity

EXPLANATION

To accomplish parity, a parity bit (equal to either 0 or 1) is added to the bits' sum.

QUESTION 171

What does parity track on a disk?

    A. Data type

    B. Data transmission method

    C. Data integrity

    D. File size

EXPLANATION

Parity does not reflect the data type, protocol, transmission method, or file size.

QUESTION 172

What is a disadvantage of RAID level 3?

    A. It does not provide a high data transfer rate when reading from the disk

    B. Parity information appears on a single disk

    C. It does not provide a high data transfer rate when writing to the disk

    D. It is not suited for video editing

EXPLANATION

RAID level 3 presents a potential single point of failure in the system.

QUESTION 173

What is the most popular data storage technique in use today?

    A. Disk stripping with distributed parity

    B. Disk mirroring

    C. Disk stripping with parity ECC

    D. Disk duplexing

EXPLANATION

The highly fault-tolerant RAID level 5 is the most popular data storage technique in use today.

QUESTION 174

What is one advantage of RAID level 5 over RAID level 3?

A. RAID level 5 does not use parity information
B. Parity information is written in one disk only
C. It is more fault tolerant
D. None of the above

EXPLANATION

Unlike RAID level 3, RAID level 5 uses several disks for parity information.

QUESTION 175

What term refers to a specialized storage device or group of storage devices that provides centralized fault-tolerant data storage for a network?

A. Disk duplexing
B. SAN
C. RAID
D. NAS

EXPLANATION

You can think of NAS as a unique type of server dedicated to data sharing.

QUESTION 176

What is one advantage of using NAS?

A. Fast access to data
B. It can communicate directly with clients on the network
C. It is faster than SAN
D. It connects to the network through a server

EXPLANATION

The advantage to using NAS over a typical file server is that a NAS device contains its own filesystem that is optimized for saving and serving files.

QUESTION 177

What term refers to distinct networks of storage devices that communicate directly with each other and with other networks?

- **A.** Disk duplexing
- **B.** SAN
- **C.** RAID
- **D.** NAS

EXPLANATION

In a typical SAN, multiple storage devices are connected to multiple, identical servers. This type of architecture is similar to the mesh topology in WANs, the most fault-tolerant type of topology possible.

QUESTION 178

What is a popular SAN transmission method?

- **A.** Channel of Fibre
- **B.** Optic Channel
- **C.** Channel of Fiber
- **D.** Fibre Channel

EXPLANATION

Fibre Channel connects devices within the SAN and also connects the SAN to other networks.

QUESTION 179

What term refers to a copy of data or program files created for archiving or safekeeping?

- **A.** Duplexing
- **B.** Mirroring
- **C.** Backup
- **D.** Self-replication

EXPLANATION

Without backing up your data, you risk losing everything through a hard disk fault, fire, flood, or malicious or accidental erasure or corruption.

QUESTION 180

What is the name for a type of media capable of storing digitized data and that uses a laser to write data to it and read data from it?

   A. Tape
   B. Optical media
   C. Disk drives
   D. Pen drives

EXPLANATION

Examples of optical media include all types of CD-ROMs and DVDs.

4

QUESTION 181

To what type of backup media does a CompactFlash card belong?

   A. Tape
   B. Optical media
   C. External disk drives
   D. Network backup

EXPLANATION

Another option for backing up data is to use an external disk drive, a storage device that can be attached temporarily to a computer via its USB, PCMCIA, FireWire, or CompactFlash port.

QUESTION 182

What backup method copies all data on all servers regardless of whether the data is new or changed?

   A. Full backup
   B. Incremental backup
   C. Decremented backup
   D. Differential backup

EXPLANATION

After backing up the files, a full backup unchecks—or turns "off"—the files' archive bits.

QUESTION 183

What is the name for a specialized device, or a computer installed with specialized software, that selectively filters or blocks traffic between networks?

    A. Wireless access point
    B. Switch
    C. Hub
    D. Firewall

EXPLANATION

A firewall typically involves a combination of hardware and software and may reside between two interconnected private networks or, more typically, between a private network and a public network.

QUESTION 184

What is the simplest form of a firewall?

    A. Proxy service
    B. Packet filtering
    C. Application gateway
    D. Application proxy

EXPLANATION

The simplest form of a firewall is a router (or a computer installed with software that enables it to act as a router) that examines the header of every packet of data it receives to determine whether that type of packet is authorized to continue to its destination.

QUESTION 185

What is the name for a software application on a network host that acts as an intermediary between the external and internal networks, screening all incoming and outgoing traffic?

    A. Firewall
    B. Router
    C. Proxy service
    D. IP Table

EXPLANATION

One approach to enhancing the security of the Network and Transport layers provided by firewalls is to combine a packet-filtering firewall with a proxy service.

QUESTION 186

What is one of the proxy service's most important functions?

    A. Logically divide a network

    B. Filter password information

    C. Prevent the internal network from discovering the outside world

    D. Prevent the outside world from discovering the addresses of the internal network

EXPLANATION

Although a proxy server appears to the outside world as an internal network server, in reality it is merely another filtering device for the internal LAN.

4

QUESTION 187

What feature allows proxy servers to improve performance for users accessing resources external to their network?

    A. Password filtering

    B. File caching

    C. Mail filtering

    D. Port filtering

EXPLANATION

For example, a proxy server situated between a LAN and an external Web server can be configured to save recently viewed Web pages. The next time a user on the LAN wants to view one of the saved Web pages, content is provided by the proxy server.

QUESTION 188

What should you consider when working with remote access?

    A. Security risks

    B. Data backup

    C. Server backup

    D. Data storage filtering

EXPLANATION

If an employee can get to your network in New York from his hotel room in Rome, a smart hacker can likely do the same.

QUESTION 189

What is one remote access method?

A. Routers

B. Firewalls

C. Server mirroring

D. Remote control systems

EXPLANATION

Remote control systems enable a user to connect to a host system on a network from a distance and use that system's resources as if the user were sitting in front of it.

QUESTION 190

What security feature should be included in a remote control system?

A. Data backup

B. Antivirus

C. Call back

D. External drives

EXPLANATION

A remote control system should enable a remote user to dial into the network, enter a user name, and hang up. The host system then calls the user back at a predetermined number.

QUESTION 191

What remote access method requires users to dial into a remote access server attached to the network?

A. Dial-up networking

B. Routers

C. Remote control system

D. Call back

EXPLANATION

Dial-up networking differs from remote control in that it effectively turns a remote workstation into a node on the network, through a remote access server.

QUESTION 192

What are the rights conferred to all users called?
- **A.** Private rights
- **B.** Public rights
- **C.** Shared rights
- **D.** Restricted rights

EXPLANATION

Anyone can have public rights, and exercising them presents no security threat to the network.

4

QUESTION 193

What action simplifies the process of granting rights to users?
- **A.** Creating groups
- **B.** Installing antivirus
- **C.** Using personal firewall
- **D.** Enabling external drives

EXPLANATION

Network administrators need to group users according to their security levels and assign additional rights that meet the needs of those groups.

QUESTION 194

What logon restriction will allow some user accounts to be valid only during specific hours?
- **A.** Unsuccessful logon attempts
- **B.** Source address
- **C.** Total time logged on
- **D.** Time of day

EXPLANATION

Specifying valid hours for an account can increase security by preventing any account from being used by unauthorized personnel after hours.

QUESTION 195

What logon restriction will set a limit on how many consecutive unsuccessful logon attempts from a single user ID the server will accept before blocking that ID from even attempting to log on?

    A. Unsuccessful logon attempts

    B. Source address

    C. Total time logged on

    D. Time of day

EXPLANATION

The unsuccessful logon attempts restriction prevents hackers from repeatedly attempting to log on under a valid username for which they do not know the password.

QUESTION 196

What is the term for the use of an algorithm to scramble data into a format that can be read only by reversing the algorithm?

    A. Scrambling

    B. Decryption

    C. Encryption

    D. Obscuring

EXPLANATION

The purpose of encryption is to keep information private.

QUESTION 197

The scrambled data is known as:

    A. Plaintext

    B. Ciphertext

    C. Normal text

    D. Random text

EXPLANATION

The longer the key, the less easily the ciphertext can be decrypted by an unauthorized system.

QUESTION 198

In what kind of encryption is data encrypted using a single key that only the sender and the receiver know?

    A. Public-private

    B. Asymmetric

    C. Public key

    D. Private key

EXPLANATION

Private key encryption is also known as symmetric encryption because the same key is used during both the transmission and reception of the data.

4

QUESTION 199

In what kind of encryption is data encrypted using two keys: One is a key known only to a user (that is, a private key), and the other is a public key associated with the user?

    A. Normal

    B. Symmetric

    C. Public key

    D. Private key

EXPLANATION

Because public key encryption requires the use of two different keys, it is also known as asymmetric encryption.

QUESTION 200

On what version of Microsoft Windows is MS-CHAPv2 supported?

    A. Windows Server 2003

    B. Windows 95

    C. Windows Me

    D. Windows for Groups

EXPLANATION

MS-CHAPv2 is available for use with VPN connections in the Windows 98, NT 4.0, 2000, XP, and Server 2003 operating systems.

ANSWER GRID FOR CORE DOMAIN 3

Question	Answer	Objective	Question	Answer	Objective
1	C	3.2	36	A	3.4
2	B	3.2	37	D	3.4
3	A	3.2	38	B	3.4
4	D	3.1	39	A	3.4
5	D	3.2	40	B	3.4
6	B	3.2	41	C, D	3.4
7	C	3.2	42	A	3.4
8	A	3.2	43	A	3.9
9	C	3.2	44	B	3.9
10	B	3.2	45	B	3.9
11	D	3.2	46	C	3.9
12	B	3.2	47	D	3.3
13	C	3.2	48	C	3.3
14	A	3.1	49	A	3.3
15	D	3.1	50	B	3.3
16	B	3.1	51	D	3.3
17	C	3.1	52	D	3.3
18	D	3.1	53	C	3.3
19	A	3.1	54	B	3.3
20	B	3.1	55	A	3.3
21	B	3.4	56	B	3.3
22	C	3.4	57	D	3.3
23	A	3.4	58	A, B	3.3
24	B	3.4	59	B	3.3
25	D	3.4	60	C, D	3.3
26	A	3.4	61	C	3.3
27	C	3.1	62	D	3.3
28	B	3.1	63	A	3.3
29	D	3.1	64	A	3.3
30	A	3.1	65	C	3.3
31	C	3.1	66	D	3.3
32	B	3.1	67	D	3.3
33	D	3.1	68	B	3.3
34	B	3.4	69	B	3.3
35	C	3.4	70	A	3.3

Question	Answer	Objective	Question	Answer	Objective
71	A	3.11	106	B	3.10
72	D	3.11	107	C	3.10
73	B	3.11	108	A	3.10
74	C	3.11	109	D	3.10
75	B	3.11	110	C	3.10
76	A	3.11	111	B	3.11
77	D	3.11	112	A	3.11
78	C	3.11	113	C	3.11
79	B	3.11	114	D	3.11
80	D	3.11	115	B	3.11
81	A	3.11	116	C	3.11
82	C, D	3.11	117	A	3.11
83	B, C	3.11	118	D	3.11
84	D	3.11	119	C	3.11
85	A	3.11	120	B	3.11
86	C	3.11	121	B	3.11
87	B	3.11	122	A	3.11
88	A, C	3.11	123	D	3.11
89	D	3.11	124	C	3.11
90	B	3.11	125	B	3.11
91	C	3.10	126	A	3.11
92	A	3.10	127	D	3.11
93	B	3.10	128	C	3.11
94	D	3.10	129	B	3.11
95	C	3.10	130	A, D	3.11
96	C	3.10	131	D	3.11
97	A	3.10	132	C	3.11
98	B	3.10	133	D	3.11
99	C	3.10	134	B	3.11
100	D	3.10	135	A	3.11
101	C	3.10	136	B, C	3.11
102	B	3.10	137	D	3.11
103	A	3.10	138	C	3.11
104	C	3.10	139	A	3.11
105	D	3.10	140	B	3.11

4

Question	Answer	Objective		Question	Answer	Objective
141	B	3.11		171	C	3.11
142	C	3.11		172	B	3.11
143	D	3.11		173	A	3.11
144	A	3.11		174	C	3.11
145	C	3.11		175	D	3.11
146	A	3.11		176	A	3.11
147	B	3.11		177	B	3.11
148	A, C	3.11		178	D	3.12
149	D	3.11		179	C	3.12
150	B	3.11		180	B	3.12
151	C	3.11		181	C	3.12
152	A	3.11		182	A	3.5
153	C	3.11		183	D	3.5
154	B	3.11		184	B	3.5
155	D	3.11		185	C	3.6
156	A	3.11		186	D	3.6, 3.7
157	B	3.11		187	B	3.6, 3.7
158	A	3.11		188	A	3.7
159	C	3.11		189	D	3.7
160	D	3.11		190	C	3.7
161	A	3.11		191	A	3.7
162	C	3.11		192	B	3.1
163	B	3.11		193	A	3.1
164	A	3.11		194	D	3.1
165	D	3.11		195	A	3.1
166	B	3.11		196	C	3.7
167	C	3.11		197	B	3.7
168	A	3.11		198	D	3.7
169	D	3.11		199	C	3.7
170	D	3.11		200	A	3.4

5

DOMAIN 4: NETWORK SUPPORT

All questions in this chapter pertain to Domain 4, Network Support, of the CompTIA Network+® exam. This domain represents 35% of the total exam and has nine sub-objectives.

For more in-depth information about this domain, see Appendix A, "Network+ (2005) Examination Objectives."

5

QUESTION 1

One of the most common transmission flaws affecting data signals is:

A. noise

B. heat

C. humidity

D. wind

EXPLANATION

Noise is any undesirable influence that may degrade or distort a signal.

QUESTION 2

A common source of noise is:

A. wavelength

B. frequency

C. electromagnetic interference (EMI)

D. amplitude

EXPLANATION

When EMI noise affects analog signals, this distortion can result in the incorrect transmission of data, just as if static prevented you from hearing a radio station broadcast.

QUESTION 3

What type of signal is more resilient to noise caused by electromagnetic interference (EMI)?

A. Analog signals
B. Broadband signals
C. Baseband signals
D. Digital signal

EXPLANATION

Because digital signals do not depend on subtle amplitude or frequency differences to communicate information, they are more apt to be readable despite distortions caused by EMI noise.

QUESTION 4

Noise caused when a signal traveling on one wire or cable infringes on the signal traveling over an adjacent wire or cable is known as:

A. Chat
B. Crosstalk
C. Intermission
D. Blocking

EXPLANATION

If you have ever been on the phone and heard the conversation on your second line in the background, you have heard the effects of crosstalk.

QUESTION 5

Another type of transmission flaw is:

A. Amplification
B. Repetition
C. Attenuation
D. Regeneration

EXPLANATION

Attenuation is the loss of a signal's strength as it travels away from its source.

QUESTION 6

To fight against attenuation with analog signals we use:
- **A.** regenerators
- **B.** repeaters
- **C.** reducers
- **D.** amplifiers

EXPLANATION

Analog signals pass through an amplifier, an electronic device that increases the voltage, or strength, of the signals.

QUESTION 7

To fight against attenuation with digital signals we use:
- **A.** regenerators
- **B.** repeaters
- **C.** reducers
- **D.** amplifiers

EXPLANATION

Repeaters are the connectivity devices that perform the regeneration of a digital signal.

QUESTION 8

When this type of signal is amplified, the noise that it has accumulated is also amplified:
- **A.** analog
- **B.** digital
- **C.** broadband
- **D.** baseband

EXPLANATION

Indiscriminate amplification causes the analog signal to worsen progressively. After multiple amplifications, an analog signal may become difficult to decipher.

5

QUESTION 9

When this type of signal is repeated, it is actually retransmitted in its original form, without the noise it may have accumulated previously:

A. analog
B. digital
C. broadband
D. baseband

EXPLANATION

This process is known as regeneration.

QUESTION 10

Amplifiers and repeaters belong to what OSI Model layer?

A. Session
B. Data Link
C. Physical
D. Transport

EXPLANATION

Amplifiers and repeaters belong to the Physical layer of the OSI Model. Both are used to extend the length of a network.

QUESTION 11

The delay between the transmission of a signal and its eventual receipt is called:

A. traveling
B. latency
C. noise
D. attenuation

EXPLANATION

Although electrons travel rapidly, they still have to travel, and a brief delay takes place between the moment you press the key and the moment the server accepts the data. This delay is called latency.

QUESTION 12

When you connect multiple network segments, the latency in the network is:

    A. decreased

    B. the same

    C. increased and decreased at the same time

    D. increased

EXPLANATION

When you connect multiple network segments, you increase the distance between sender and receiver.

QUESTION 13

The type of media least susceptible to noise is:

    A. coaxial cable

    B. copper cable

    C. fiber-optic cable

    D. UTP cable

EXPLANATION

Fiber-optic cable does not use electric current, but light waves, to conduct signals.

QUESTION 14

These types of signals are more apt to be distorted by EMI/RFI than signals traveling over a cable:

    A. wireless

    B. broadband

    C. baseband

    D. broadcast

EXPLANATION

Wireless signals are more apt to be distorted by EMI/RFI than signals traveling over a cable.

QUESTION 15

What is the command to view IP information on a Windows XP workstation?

A. ifconfig
B. ipconfig
C. netstat
D. arp -a

EXPLANATION

At the command prompt on a Windows XP workstation, type **ipconfig /all** and press Enter. Your workstation's IP address information is displayed.

QUESTION 16

What is the command to view IP information on a Linux workstation?

A. ifconfig
B. ipconfig
C. netstat
D. arp -a

EXPLANATION

On a Linux operating system, simply type **ifconfig -a** at the shell prompt to view all the information about your TCP/IP connections and addresses.

QUESTION 17

What is the name of a utility that can verify that TCP/IP is installed, bound to the NIC, configured correctly, and communicating with the network?

A. PING
B. Loopback
C. Loopback test
D. Echo test

EXPLANATION

PING uses ICMP services to send echo request and echo reply messages that determine the validity of an IP address.

QUESTION 18

What is the name of the service that decides if a client's request must be attended by the client itself or the server?

A. Router

B. Analyzer

C. Redirector

D. Proxy

EXPLANATION

A service on the client workstation called the redirector intercepts a client's request to determine whether it should be handled by the client or by the server.

QUESTION 19

If after entering her name and password a user receives an error message indicating that the server was not found, this suggest a problem in what layer of the OSI Model?

A. Data Link

B. Physical

C. Network

D. Application

EXPLANATION

In this case a physical connection problem may be at fault.

QUESTION 20

What can you do to expedite access to directories whose files you frequently require on a remote machine?

A. Create favorites

B. Write down the resource address for easy access

C. Do not ask for a username and password

D. Map a drive to a directory

EXPLANATION

Mapping involves associating a letter, such as M: or T:, with a disk, directory, or other resource (such as a CD-ROM tower).

QUESTION 21

What file access protocol do Windows Server 2003 and Windows XP clients use to communicate with each other?

A. AES
B. NFS
C. Common Internet File System
D. Novell File System

EXPLANATION

CIFS is a more recent version of an older client-server communication protocol, Server Message Block (SMB), which originated at IBM and then was adopted and further developed by Microsoft.

QUESTION 22

What is the name of the utility that displays TCP/IP statistics and details about TCP/IP components and connections on a host?

A. netinfo
B. netfiles
C. netstat
D. netcfg

EXPLANATION

Information that can be obtained from netstat includes the port number for a particular running TCP/IP service, whether or not a remote node is logged, and network connections currently established for a client, among others.

QUESTION 23

Netstat can be used as a:

A. Diagnostic tool
B. Visualization tool
C. Interactive tool
D. Routing tool

EXPLANATION

With so much statistical information available, the netstat utility makes a powerful diagnostic tool.

QUESTION 24

What is true about the netstat command?

    A. It allows switching variables

    B. It does not allow switching variables

    C. netstat –a is the only available switching variable

    D. netstat –r is the only available switching variable

EXPLANATION

Like other TCP/IP commands, netstat can be used with a number of different switches.

QUESTION 25

Which one is a correct example of a netstat command?

    A. –a netstat

    B. netstat –a

    C. netstat /a

    D. netstat :a

EXPLANATION

A netstat command begins with the word netstat followed by a space, then a hyphen and a switch, followed by a variable pertaining to that switch, if required.

QUESTION 26

What is true about NetBIOS?

    A. NetBIOS alone is routable

    B. Even when combined with TCP/IP, NetBIOS is not routable

    C. NetBIOS alone is not routable

    D. NetBIOS does not need to be routable

EXPLANATION

NetBIOS is a protocol that runs in the Session and Transport layers of the OSI Model.

QUESTION 27

What is the name of the utility that provides information about NetBIOS statistics and resolves NetBIOS names to their IP addresses?

- **A.** netstat
- **B.** nbiostat
- **C.** netbiost
- **D.** nbtstat

EXPLANATION

If you know the NetBIOS name of a workstation, you can use nbtstat to determine its IP address.

QUESTION 28

On what kind of networks is nbtstat useful?

- **A.** Linux-based networks
- **B.** Windows-based networks
- **C.** UNIX-based networks
- **D.** Novell networks

EXPLANATION

Because Novell and UNIX types of operating systems do not use NetBIOS, nbtstat is not useful on these types of networks.

QUESTION 29

What is true about the nbtstat command?

- **A.** Switching variables are case sensitive
- **B.** Unlike netstat, it does not allow switching variables
- **C.** Switching variables are not case sensitive
- **D.** −a is the only valid switching variable

EXPLANATION

For nbtstat, the -a switch has a different meaning than the -A switch.

QUESTION 30

What is the correct nbtstat command format to determine what machine is registered to a given IP address?

    A. nbtstat −i ip_address

    B. nbtstat −r ip_address

    C. nbtstat −a ip_address

    D. nbtstat −A ip_address

EXPLANATION

The −A switch displays a machine's name table given its IP address; the IP address of the machine must be supplied after the -A switch.

QUESTION 31

What is the name of the utility that allows you to query the DNS database from any computer on the network and find the hostname of a device by specifying its IP address, or vice versa?

    A. dnslookup

    B. dnsfind

    C. nslookup

    D. nsfind

EXPLANATION

If you wanted to find out whether the host whose name is ftp.netscape.com is operational, you could type **nslookup ftp.netscape.com** and press Enter.

QUESTION 32

What is the correct command to find the hostname of a device whose IP address you know?

    A. netstat −a ip_address

    B. nslookup ip_address

    C. nslookup −A ip_address

    D. nbtstat −A ip_address

EXPLANATION

Using the nslookup command along with an IP address, you can determine the hostname associated with that address.

QUESTION 33

What happens when you type **nslookup** alone and then press Enter?

- **A.** You will be prompted for additional commands
- **B.** You will get an error message
- **C.** You will get all DNS information from your server
- **D.** You will get information from all NICs in your network

EXPLANATION

Typing just nslookup (without any switches) and then pressing Enter starts the nslookup utility, and the command prompt changes to a >.

QUESTION 34

dig is similar to this other TCP/IP utility:

- **A.** finger
- **B.** netstat
- **C.** nbtstat
- **D.** nslookup

EXPLANATION

dig allows you to query a DNS database and find the hostname associated with a specific IP address or vice versa.

QUESTION 35

What is one difference between dig and nslookup?

- **A.** nslookup provided more detailed information
- **B.** dig provides more detailed information
- **C.** dig does not accept an IP address as a switch variable
- **D.** nslookup does not accept a hostname as a switch variable

EXPLANATION

While the simple nslookup command returns the IP address for a hostname, the simple dig command returns specifics about the resource records associated with that hostname.

QUESTION 36

What is one difference between dig and nslookup?

    A. nslookup does not allow switches variables

    B. dig does not allow switches variables

    C. nslookup is more flexible than dig

    D. dig is more flexible than nslookup

EXPLANATION

The dig utility comes with over two dozen switches.

QUESTION 37

What is true about the dig command?

    A. It works only for UNIX-based DNS servers

    B. It is included with Windows-type operating systems

    C. It is included with UNIX-type operating systems

    D. It works only for Windows-based DNS servers

EXPLANATION

If your computer runs a Windows-based operating system, you must obtain the code for the dig utility from a third party and install it on your system.

QUESTION 38

What is the name of the utility that allows you to query a DNS registration database and obtain information about a domain?

    A. finger

    B. whois

    C. ping

    D. lsuser

EXPLANATION

Using whois can help troubleshoot network problems. For example, if you noticed your network received a flood of messages that originated from www.trinketmakers.com, you could find out who leases the trinketmakers.com domain and contact them about the problem.

QUESTION 39

Syntax of the whois command is whois xxx.yy. To what level of the domain name does xxx.yy belong?

    A. First level

    B. Second level

    C. Third level

    D. Fourth level

EXPLANATION

You could type **whois trinketmakers.com** at a UNIX shell prompt to obtain the registration information for www.trinketmakers.com.

QUESTION 40

What is true about the whois command?

    A. You can use a Web-based interface to run it

    B. It can only be run at the shell or command prompt

    C. It can only be run on a UNIX-based operating system

    D. It is only available for Windows-based servers

EXPLANATION

Rather than type whois at the shell or command prompt, however, you might prefer to use one of the many Web sites that provide simple, Web-based interfaces for running the whois command.

QUESTION 41

What is the name of the utility used to trace the path from one networked node to another, identifying all intermediate hops between the two nodes? (Choose 2)

    A. hello

    B. ping

    C. traceroute

    D. tracert

EXPLANATION

The traceroute utility (known as tracert on Windows-based systems) is useful for determining router or subnet connectivity problems.

QUESTION 42

What kind of datagrams does traceroute use?

    A. SPX

    B. IPX

    C. TCP

    D. UDP

EXPLANATION

The traceroute utility uses ICMP to trace the path from one networked node to another, identifying all intermediate hops between the two nodes.

QUESTION 43

5

To find a route, traceroute uses the destination: (Choose 2)

    A. IP address

    B. Hostname

    C. MAC address

    D. Subnet mask

EXPLANATION

To find the route, the traceroute utility transmits a series of UDP datagrams to a specified destination, using either the IP address or the hostname to identify the destination.

QUESTION 44

What happens with the TTL field on a traceroute datagram?

    A. It is fixed at 1

    B. It is fixed at 2

    C. It is increased by 1 every time a router in the path is found

    D. It is increased by 2 every time a router in the path is found

EXPLANATION

The first datagrams in traceroute have a TTL of 1. After it learns about the first router in the path, it transmits datagrams with a TTL of 2. The process continues for the next router in the path and then the third, fourth, and so on until the destination node is reached.

QUESTION 45

What are two reasons why a traceroute test may fail?

    A. Destination host uses a Windows-based operating system

    B. Destination host is down

    C. Destination host is a Linux server

    D. Destination host is behind a firewall

EXPLANATION

A traceroute test may stop before reaching the destination, however. This happens for one of two reasons: Either the device that traceroute is attempting to reach is down or it does not accept ICMP transmissions.

QUESTION 46

What is the winipcfg equivalent command for Windows NT, 2000, XP, and Server 2003 operating systems?

    A. ipconfig

    B. ifconfig

    C. ipcfg

    D. wntipcfg

EXPLANATION

Ipconfig is a command-line utility that provides information about a network adapter's IP address, subnet mask, and default gateway.

QUESTION 47

What is the appropriate command to view complete information about your TCP/IP settings on a Windows XP workstation?

    A. ifconfig -a

    B. ipconfig –all

    C. ipconfig /all

    D. ipcfg /all

EXPLANATION

With ipconfig, a forward slash (/) precedes the command switches, rather than a hyphen.

QUESTION 48

What is the name of the TCP/IP administration utility for use with the Windows Me operating system?

    A. ipconfig

    B. ifconfig

    C. ipcfg

    D. winipcfg

EXPLANATION

The winipcfg utility performs the same TCP/IP configuration and management as the ipconfig utility but applies to Windows 9x and Me operating systems.

QUESTION 49

How can you manage TCP/IP settings on a UNIX-type operating system?

    A. ipconfig

    B. ifconfig

    C. ipcfg

    D. winipcfg

EXPLANATION

As with ipconfig on Windows NT/2000/XP/2003 systems and winipcfg on Windows 9x systems, ifconfig enables you to manage TCP/IP settings on UNIX-type systems.

QUESTION 50

Select a correct example of an ifconfig command:

    A. ifconfig –a

    B. ifconfig a

    C. ifconfig -down

    D. ifconfig -up

EXPLANATION

The switch –a applies the command to all interfaces on a device and can be used with other switches.

5

QUESTION 51

What should be the first step when troubleshooting a network?

A. Solve the problem using the same solution as last time

B. Rewire the network

C. Identify what is wrong with the network

D. Reset your connectivity devices

EXPLANATION

You should always try to identify the symptoms and potential causes of the problem before fixing it.

QUESTION 52

What is a good troubleshooting technique?

A. Assume the problem affects the whole network

B. Identify the affected area

C. Assume the problem affects only you

D. Routers are never the cause of network problems

EXPLANATION

Are users across the entire network experiencing the problem at all times? Or is the problem limited to a specific geographic area of the network, to a specific demographic group of users, or to a particular period of time?

QUESTION 53

When there is a problem with your network, you should check for:

A. Changes in your administrator privileges

B. Changes with the TCP/IP utility tools

C. Default configuration options

D. Recent changes in the network configuration

EXPLANATION

When troubleshooting, you should also establish what has changed. Recent hardware or software changes may be causing the symptoms.

QUESTION 54

What are probable causes of a network failure?

    A. Logical integrity

    B. Physical integrity

    C. Users

    D. All of the above

EXPLANATION

User competency and physical and logical integrity of the network are probable causes of network problems.

QUESTION 55

What should you do after you successfully solve a network problem?

    A. Document everything

    B. Just forget about it

    C. Do nothing

    D. None of the above

EXPLANATION

Document the solution and process. Make sure that both you and your colleagues understand the cause of the problem and how you solved it.

QUESTION 56

Select a true statement about network troubleshooting:

    A. You first identify the causes of a problem

    B. You first identify the problem, then the causes

    C. You troubleshoot a problem without identifying its causes

    D. You identify a problem's symptoms by its causes

EXPLANATION

When troubleshooting a network problem, your first step is to identify the specific symptoms of the problem. After you identify the problem's symptoms, you can begin to deduce its cause.

QUESTION 57

What is a potential danger when troubleshooting your network?

A. Treating each symptom as unique

B. Treating each user report about a problem as unique

C. Jumping to conclusions about the symptoms

D. Paying too much attention to network behavior

EXPLANATION

Take time to pay attention to the users, system and network behavior, and any error messages. Treat each symptom as unique (but potentially related to others). In this way, you avoid the risk of ignoring problems or—even worse—causing more problems.

QUESTION 58

What is a good troubleshooting practice?

A. If two or more users report a similar problem, treat both reports as only one symptom

B. Never print an error message screen because it may lead you to the wrong problem

C. After solving the problem, discard your notes about it

D. Take note of the error messages reported by users

EXPLANATION

If you aren't near the users, ask them to read the messages to you directly off their screens or, better yet, print the screens that contain the error messages.

QUESTION 59

When troubleshooting a problem, what is the next step after you have identified the problem's symptoms and its probable causes?

A. Establish what has changed

B. Identify the affected areas

C. Select the most probable cause

D. Test your solution

EXPLANATION

After you have identified the problem's symptoms, you should determine whether the problem affects only a certain group of users or certain areas of the organization, or if the problem occurs at certain times.

QUESTION 60

What is one advantage of identifying the affected areas when troubleshooting your network?

A. It helps you better identify the problem causes
B. Add more causes
C. Less documentation about the problem
D. All of the above

EXPLANATION

For example, if a problem affects only users on a wireless network segment, you may deduce that the problem lies with that segment's access point.

QUESTION 61

When identifying the affected areas on your network you should also pay attention to:

A. User competency
B. The most probable cause
C. The problem time frame
D. User technical skills

EXPLANATION

Discovering the time or frequency with which a problem occurs can reveal more subtle network problems.

QUESTION 62

A network failure can be a consequence of:

A. A new software installed on a server
B. Adding a new user to the network
C. A change in the operating system configuration
D. All of the above

EXPLANATION

As you begin troubleshooting, you should be aware of any recent changes to your network.

5

QUESTION 63

What can you do if you suspect that a network change has generated a problem? (Choose 2)

- **A.** Fix the problem
- **B.** Reverse the change
- **C.** Leave it to be fixed in your next troubleshooting step
- **D.** Do nothing

EXPLANATION

If you suspect that a network change has generated a problem, you can react in two ways: You can attempt to correct the problem that resulted from the change, or you can attempt to reverse the change and restore the hardware or software to its previous state.

QUESTION 64

What will help you establish what has changed on your network when troubleshooting? (Choose 2)

- **A.** Ask users about the changes
- **B.** Good documentation
- **C.** Make documentation available
- **D.** Allow users to make configuration changes

EXPLANATION

To track what has changed on a network, you and your colleagues in the IT Department should keep complete network change records. In addition to keeping thorough records, you must make them available to staff members who might need to reference them.

QUESTION 65

What is one of the first things you should eliminate as a potential cause of a network problem?

- **A.** Cabling problems
- **B.** Problems with your switches
- **C.** Problems with your routers
- **D.** Human error

EXPLANATION

As a troubleshooter, one of your first steps is to ensure that human error is not the source of the problem.

QUESTION 66

What is a good way of avoiding human errors that can lead to network problems?
- **A.** Training
- **B.** Installing a network monitor on the user's machine
- **C.** Assigning new users to the "untrained" workgroup
- **D.** All of the above

EXPLANATION

Although human problems may seem simple to solve, unless a user receives training in the proper procedures and understands what might go wrong, he will never know how to solve a problem without assistance.

QUESTION 67

Watching a user is the best way to discover a human-related problem. If watching a user is not possible, what is the next best practice?
- **A.** Ask users for a written detailed report of the problem
- **B.** Talk with users during the process that generates the problem
- **C.** Ask users to log out from the system
- **D.** Ask users to reboot their workstations

EXPLANATION

If this tactic isn't practical, the next best way is to talk with the user by phone while he tries to replicate the error. At every step, calmly ask the user to explain what appears on the screen and what, exactly, he is doing.

QUESTION 68

What practices will help you learn more about a network problem? (Choose 2)
- **A.** Checking your connectivity devices
- **B.** Checking for cabling issues
- **C.** Re-create the problem logged on as the user
- **D.** Re-create the problem logged on as administrator

EXPLANATION

An excellent way to learn more about the causes of a problem is to try to re-create the symptoms yourself.

QUESTION 69

What questions can you answer by re-creating a network problem? (Choose 2)

    A. Is the problem recurrent?

    B. Did the problem never occur?

    C. Is the problem consistent each time?

    D. Is the problem a false alarm?

EXPLANATION

Re-creating a problem helps you find answers for questions such as: Can you make the symptoms recur every time? If symptoms recur, are they consistent?

QUESTION 70

What practice should be followed when re-creating a network problem?

    A. Do not pay attention to the problem time frame when trying to reproduce it

    B. Reproduce a problem guided by its type

    C. Follow your instincts

    D. Follow the same steps that the person reporting the symptoms followed

EXPLANATION

If you attempt to reproduce a problem by performing different functions than those employed by the user, you may not be able to reproduce a legitimate problem and thus might assume that the symptoms resulted from user error.

QUESTION 71

What do physical connectivity problems include? (Choose 2)

    A. Hubs

    B. Routers

    C. NICs

    D. Switches

EXPLANATION

By some estimates, more than half of all network problems occur at the Physical layer of the OSI Model, which includes cabling, network adapters, repeaters, and hubs.

QUESTION 72

What is a good symptom of a physical connectivity problem?
- **A.** A workstation printer does not want to print
- **B.** A workstation display does not turn on
- **C.** A login error message
- **D.** Intermittent connectivity

EXPLANATION

Often, physical connectivity problems manifest as a continuous or intermittent inability to connect to the network and perform network-related functions.

QUESTION 73

5

What is a potential cause of a physical connectivity problem?
- **A.** An Ethernet 100BASE-TX segment of 50 meters
- **B.** An Ethernet 100BASE-TX segment that exceeds 100 meters
- **C.** An Ethernet 100BASE-TX segment of 20 meters
- **D.** All of the above

EXPLANATION

Causes of unreliable network connectivity may include a segment or network length that exceeds the IEEE maximum standards.

QUESTION 74

What is true about physical network problems?
- **A.** They always affect software applications
- **B.** They never affect software applications
- **C.** They might affect software applications
- **D.** Half of the time they affect software applications

EXPLANATION

Physical connectivity problems do not typically (but occasionally can) result in software application anomalies, the inability to use a single application, poor network performance, protocol errors, software licensing errors, or software usage errors.

QUESTION 75

What is an easy way to test that a problem lies with a network component?

A. Swapping equipment
B. Follow that component connection from endpoint to endpoint
C. Install the latest NOS updates for that component
D. Upgrade the component hardware

EXPLANATION

If you suspect a problem lies with a network component, one of the easiest ways to test your theory is to exchange that component for a functional one.

QUESTION 76

What is a better and more expensive alternative to swapping equipment?

A. Swapping a router
B. Equipment redundancy
C. Swapping a switch
D. Equipment upgrade

EXPLANATION

A better—albeit more expensive—alternative to swapping parts is to have redundancy built into your network.

QUESTION 77

When should you check for logical connectivity problems?

A. Before you check for physical connectivity problems
B. Instead of checking for physical connectivity problems
C. You never check for logical connectivity problems
D. After you check for physical connectivity problems

EXPLANATION

Once you have verified the physical connections, you must examine the firmware and software configurations, settings, installations, and privileges.

QUESTION 78

What kind of problem might a logical connectivity problem include?

    A. Cabling
    B. NOS
    C. Repeaters
    D. EMP interference

EXPLANATION

Depending on the type of symptoms, you may need to investigate networked applications, the network operating system, or hardware configurations, such as NIC IRQ settings. All of these elements belong in the category of "logical connectivity."

QUESTION 79

What is true about logical connectivity problems when compared against physical connectivity problems?

    A. Logical problems are easier to isolate
    B. In general both problems are very easy to identify
    C. Physical problems are easier to isolate
    D. Logical problems are easier to resolve

EXPLANATION

Logical connectivity problems often prove more difficult to isolate and resolve than physical connectivity problems because they can be more complex.

QUESTION 80

When should you think of a solution for a network problem?

    A. After you have analyzed the problem
    B. Immediately after somebody reports the problem
    C. After you have at least five reports for the same problem
    D. After the problem affects yourself

EXPLANATION

After you have thoroughly analyzed a network problem, you will be able to devise an action plan and implement your solution.

QUESTION 81

The breadth of a change is also known as:

- **A.** Consequence
- **B.** Scope
- **C.** Documentation
- **D.** Privilege

EXPLANATION

One of the most important aspects to consider is the breadth, or scope, of your change.

QUESTION 82

When should you think about the scope of your solution?

- **A.** After you have implemented the solution
- **B.** While implementing the solution
- **C.** When documenting the change
- **D.** Before implementing the solution

EXPLANATION

Assess the scope of your solution—whether it is a single workstation, a workgroup, a location, or the entire network—before implementing that solution.

QUESTION 83

Besides the scope of your solution, what else should you consider about it?

- **A.** The time it took you to figure out the solution
- **B.** Tradeoffs
- **C.** Your staff technical skills for implementing the solution
- **D.** All of the above

EXPLANATION

Along with the scope, another factor to consider is the tradeoff your solution might impose.

QUESTION 84

A solution may inadvertently allow other people to access network resources. What kind of problem is this?

   A. Scope
   B. Cost
   C. Security
   D. Tradeoff

EXPLANATION

Be aware of the security implications of your solution, because it may inadvertently result in the addition or removal of network access or resource privileges for a user or group of users.

QUESTION 85

Does your solution allow your network to grow later on? This factor is known as:

   A. Scalability
   B. Enhancement
   C. Security
   D. Cost

EXPLANATION

Also consider the scalability of the solution you intend to implement. Does it position the network for additions and enhancements later on, or is it merely a temporary fix that the organization will outgrow in a year?

QUESTION 86

Select the statement that better describes the "implementing the solution" step:

   A. It always is a very brief process
   B. It will always take a long time
   C. It does not require you to understand the problem before implementing the solution
   D. A more methodical and logical implementation will lead you to better results

EXPLANATION

Implementing a solution requires foresight and patience.

QUESTION 87

What is a good practice when implementing a solution?

    A. Take notes of big changes only

    B. Discard anything you have changed so it does not get confused with new material

    C. Always keep a copy of the previous state of whatever you are changing

    D. Take notes of complex changes only

EXPLANATION

If you are reinstalling software on a device, make a backup of the device's existing software installation. If you are changing hardware on a device, keep the old parts handy in case the solution doesn't work.

QUESTION 88

What is a good practice when making changes to your network?

    A. Discard your documentation after you test the solution

    B. Keep a log with your actions

    C. Keep documentation of successful solutions only

    D. Document big changes only

EXPLANATION

Record your actions in detail so that you can later enter the information into a database.

QUESTION 89

How should you proceed in the case of large-scale fixes?

    A. Change everything in one big step

    B. Always do things remotely

    C. Always do things locally

    D. Plan your changes in different steps

EXPLANATION

In the case of large-scale fixes—for example, applying new configurations on a global VPN's routers because of a security threat—you should roll out changes in stages.

QUESTION 90

What is the next step after implementing a solution?
- **A.** Test the solution
- **B.** Document the solution
- **C.** Discard old parts and pieces
- **D.** Destroy documentation about the process

EXPLANATION

After implementing your solution, you must test its result and verify that you have solved the problem properly.

QUESTION 91

The type of test you use depends on: (Choose 2)
- **A.** The documentation you have
- **B.** The solution itself
- **C.** The time of the day
- **D.** The affected areas

EXPLANATION

The way you test the results of your solution will depend on the solution itself and the area affected by the problem.

QUESTION 92

What is true about testing a solution?
- **A.** It is always possible to test your solution immediately after its implementation
- **B.** No matter what, you should always test your solution immediately after its implementation
- **C.** It is not always possible to test a solution immediately after its implementation
- **D.** You should always wait a reasonable period of time before testing your solution

EXPLANATION

In some cases, you may have to wait days or weeks before you know for certain whether a solution worked.

QUESTION 93

What should you do immediately after testing a solution?

- **A.** Determine why it works
- **B.** Document the solution
- **C.** Discard old parts and pieces
- **D.** Destroy documentation about the process

EXPLANATION

Upon testing your solution, you should be able to determine how and why the solution was successful and what effects it had on users and functionality.

QUESTION 94

What should you do immediately after identifying the results and effects of your solution?

- **A.** Analyze the problem symptoms
- **B.** Share your knowledge
- **C.** Talk to the users
- **D.** Take notes about the process

EXPLANATION

After you have implemented and tested your solution and identified its results and effects, communicate your solution to your colleagues, thus adding to the store of knowledge about your network.

QUESTION 95

It is always a good idea to create a centrally located documentation:

- **A.** Record
- **B.** Log
- **C.** Book
- **D.** Database

EXPLANATION

An effective way to document problems and solutions is in a centrally located database to which all networking personnel have online access.

QUESTION 96

Commonly, what is the first place users call to report errors?

    A. Network administrator office

    B. IT Department

    C. Help desk

    D. Network administrator secretary

EXPLANATION

Many staff members may contribute to troubleshooting a network problem. Often the division of duties is formalized, with a help desk acting as the first, single point of contact for users to call regarding errors.

QUESTION 97

What is typically the level of expertise in workstation and network troubleshooting for people on a help desk?

    A. Basic

    B. Intermediate

    C. Advanced

    D. Expert

EXPLANATION

A help desk is typically staffed with help desk analysts—people proficient in basic (but not usually advanced) workstation and network troubleshooting.

QUESTION 98

At what support level may a help desk coordinator serve?

    A. First

    B. Second

    C. Third

    D. Fourth

EXPLANATION

A help desk coordinator may also take responsibility for troubleshooting a problem when the second-level support analyst is unable to solve it.

QUESTION 99

What is the name of the software application some organizations used for documenting problems?

    A. Call forwarding system

    B. Call tracking system

    C. Call errors database

    D. Call information center

EXPLANATION

A call tracking system is also informally known as help desk software.

QUESTION 100

What field should a typical problem record form include?

    A. Who resolved the problem last time

    B. When was this problem reported last time

    C. If this problem was solved before

    D. When the problem was first noticed

EXPLANATION

A typical problem record form should include information about the problem symptoms, including when it was first noticed.

QUESTION 101

What field is the name of the document that lists every service and software package supported within an organization, plus the names of first- and second-level support contacts for those services or software packages?

    A. Supported service list

    B. Service directory

    C. Supported list

    D. Supported directory

EXPLANATION

Your department should take responsibility for managing a supported services list that help desk personnel can use as a reference.

QUESTION 102

Communicating problems and solutions to your peers whenever you work on a network problem is not enough. What else should you do?

    A. Prune the documentation database

    B. Follow up with the user who reported the problem

    C. Delete sensitive information from the documentation database

    D. None of the above

EXPLANATION

Make sure that the user understands how or why the problem occurred, what you did to resolve the problem, and whom to contact should the problem recur.

QUESTION 103

What is the name of a process or program that provides support personnel with a centralized means of documenting changes to the network?

    A. Change database

    B. Change tracking system

    C. Call tracking system

    D. Change management system

EXPLANATION

A change management system may be as simple as one document on the network to which networking personnel continually add entries to mark their changes.

5

QUESTION 104

What type of network changes should be recorded in the change management system? (Choose 2)

    A. Password changes

    B. A new group of users is created

    C. Software changes

    D. Hardware changes

EXPLANATION

The types of changes that network personnel should record in a change management system include among others: adding or upgrading hardware or software on a network component.

QUESTION 105

What is the name of the tool that inspects network traffic?

    A. Network monitor

    B. Network controller

    C. Network agent

    D. Network administrator system

EXPLANATION

A network monitor is a software-based tool that continually monitors network traffic from a server or workstation attached to the network.

QUESTION 106

Network monitors can interpret up to what layer of the OSI Model?

    A. 2

    B. 3

    C. 5

    D. 7

EXPLANATION

A network monitor can determine the protocols passed by each frame, but it can't interpret the data inside the frame.

QUESTION 107

Who is the developer of the network monitor application NETMON?

    A. Microsoft

    B. Cisco

    C. Novell

    D. Lynksis

EXPLANATION

NETMON is a NetWare Loadable Module (NLM) that comes with NetWare 5.x and 6.x.

QUESTION 108

In what mode will a network adapter card "listen" to all traffic passing over the network?
A. Stealth
B. Advanced
C. Normal
D. Promiscuous

EXPLANATION

In promiscuous mode, a device driver directs the network adapter card to pick up all frames that pass over the network—not just those destined for the node served by the card.

QUESTION 109

5

What listening mode should the NIC of the network monitor use?
A. Promiscuous
B. Advanced
C. Privileged
D. Auditing

EXPLANATION

To take advantage of network monitoring and analyzing tools, the network adapter installed in the machine running the software must hear all traffic passing over the network.

QUESTION 110

What is a basic function of a network monitoring tool?
A. Discover all network nodes on a segment
B. Store traffic data and generate reports
C. Capture traffic generated or received by a particular node
D. Establish a normal behavior measure of a network

EXPLANATION

Network monitoring tools should at least capture frames sent to or from a specific node.

QUESTION 111

What is the name for the network error when several nodes transmit at the same time?

  A. Normal collision
  B. Local collision
  C. Late collision
  D. Runts

EXPLANATION

Local collisions occur when two or more stations are transmitting simultaneously.

QUESTION 112

What is the name for collisions that take place outside the window of time in which they would normally be detected by the network?

  A. Delayed collisions
  B. Local collisions
  C. Giants
  D. Late collisions

EXPLANATION

Late collisions are usually caused by a defective station that is transmitting without first verifying line status or failure to observe the configuration guidelines for cable length, which results in collisions being recognized too late.

QUESTION 113

What is the name for packets that are smaller than the medium's minimum packet size?

  A. Runts
  B. Giants
  C. Jabbers
  D. Collisions

EXPLANATION

Any Ethernet packet that is smaller than 64 bytes is an example of that.

QUESTION 114

What is the opposite of a runt?
   A. Local collision
   B. Jabber
   C. Giant
   D. Late collision

EXPLANATION

Giants are packets that exceed the medium's maximum packet size.

QUESTION 115

What is the name for a device that handles electrical signals improperly?
   A. Ghosts
   B. Jabber
   C. Runt
   D. Giant

EXPLANATION

A jabber usually results from a bad NIC. Occasionally, it can be caused by outside electrical interference.

QUESTION 116

Negative frame sequence checks are the results of two mismatching:
   A. Cyclic Redundancy Checks
   B. Electric signals
   C. Magnetic signals
   D. Frame sequence numbers

EXPLANATION

A high number of negative CRCs usually results from excessive collisions or a station transmitting bad data.

QUESTION 117

Ghosts are the result of:

   A. Mismatching CRCs
   B. Mismatching frame headers
   C. Unrecognized sequence number
   D. Unrecognized voltage

EXPLANATION

Frames that are not actually data frames, but aberrations caused by a device misinterpreting stray voltage on the wire, are called ghosts.

QUESTION 118

What is the difference between a protocol analyzer and a network monitor?

   A. Protocol analyzer can understand frames up to the Network layer of the OSI Model
   B. Protocol analyzer can understand frames up to the second layer of the OSI Model
   C. Protocol analyzer can operate at any layer of the OSI Model
   D. Protocol analyzer can understand frames up to the Transport layer of the OSI Model

EXPLANATION

A protocol analyzer can also analyze frames, typically all the way to Layer 7 of the OSI Model.

QUESTION 119

A protocol analyzer is also known as:

   A. Protocol monitor
   B. Network analyzer
   C. Network monitor
   D. Protocol checker

EXPLANATION

A protocol analyzer (or network analyzer) is another tool that can capture traffic.

QUESTION 120

What kind of tool can capture unencrypted passwords going over the network?

A. Network analyzer
B. Network monitor
C. Cable performance tester
D. Cable checker

EXPLANATION

Protocol analyzers can also interpret the payload portion of frames, translating from binary or hexadecimal code to human-readable form.

QUESTION 121

What is true about protocol analyzers?

A. They are always software-based tools
B. They are always hardware-based tools
C. They only work over a UNIX-based network
D. They can be either software-based or hardware-based tools

EXPLANATION

Sniffer Technologies has led the way in developing hardware-based protocol analyzers under the Sniffer brand name.

QUESTION 122

What is a difference between a hardware-based protocol analyzer and a laptop running a network monitoring tool?

A. Laptop cannot be used for any other purpose
B. Protocol analyzer cannot be used for any other purpose
C. Protocol analyzer can be used for other purposes
D. None of the above

EXPLANATION

Unlike laptops that have a network monitoring tool installed, hardware-based protocol analyzers typically don't depend on a familiar desktop operating system such as Windows.

QUESTION 123

What is an advantage that hardware-based protocol analyzers have over network monitors?

    A. Protocol analyzers can be used for other purposes

    B. Protocol analyzers uses familiar desktop operating systems

    C. Protocol analyzers can capture more information from the NIC

    D. All of the above

EXPLANATION

Because they do not rely on a desktop operating system such as Windows, hardware-based network analyzers do not rely on Windows device drivers (for the NIC).

QUESTION 124

What can be a disadvantage in using protocol analyzers?

    A. They can collect too much information

    B. They do not collect enough information

    C. They do not allow information filtering

    D. They do not allow filters based on MAC addresses

EXPLANATION

Protocol analyzers offer a great deal of versatility in the type and depth of information they can reveal. The danger in using this type of tool is that it may collect more information than you or the machine can reasonably process.

QUESTION 125

What kind of network component has made network monitoring more difficult?

    A. Switch

    B. Router

    C. Hub

    D. Repeater

EXPLANATION

A switch logically separates a network into different segments. If a network is fully switched, your protocol analyzer can capture only frames destined for the port to which your node is connected.

QUESTION 126

What should you do before using a network monitor or protocol analyzer tool?

    A. Label all your cables

    B. Get familiar with your network traffic

    C. Shut down your servers

    D. Unplug the cable from its NIC

EXPLANATION

Before using a network monitor or protocol analyzer on a network, it's important to know what traffic on your network normally looks like.

QUESTION 127

What kind of tool can you use to monitor your wireless network?

    A. Cable continuity testers

    B. Network analyzers

    C. Network monitors

    D. None of the above

EXPLANATION

For that you will need tools that contain wireless NICs and run wireless protocols.

QUESTION 128

What is the most basic way to learn something about a wireless network?

    A. Checking the properties of your Ethernet connection

    B. Using a cable continuity tester

    C. Checking your own connection properties

    D. Using a network monitor

EXPLANATION

You can learn some things about a wireless environment by viewing the wireless network connection properties on your workstation.

QUESTION 129

What information about a wireless network can you discover using a wireless network tester?

    A. If somebody is using a network analyzer

    B. If somebody is using a network monitor

    C. Ethernet packets

    D. APs in the area

EXPLANATION

Many programs exist that can scan for wireless signals over a certain geographical range and discover all the APs and wireless stations transmitting in the area.

QUESTION 130

What is the name of a tool that can assess the quality of the wireless signal?

    A. Spectrum analyzer

    B. Multimeter

    C. Network monitor

    D. Ohmmeter

EXPLANATION

Spectrum analysis is useful, for example, to ascertain where noise (or interference) is greatest.

QUESTION 131

What kind of wireless network tester tools can you find on the market?

    A. Software-based only

    B. Both software and hardware

    C. Hardware-based only

    D. Only for Windows-based NOS

EXPLANATION

Some companies have created testing instruments whose sole purpose is to assess the status of wireless networks.

QUESTION 132

What is one advantage of hardware-based wireless network testers?

A. Cost

B. Portability

C. Security

D. Efficiency

EXPLANATION

One advantage to using such devices, however, is that they are typically more portable than a laptop or desktop workstation.

QUESTION 133

What is one advantage that a hardware-based wireless network tester has over a wireless-capable laptop?

A. The laptop's NIC is more secure

B. The laptop's NIC has a more powerful antenna

C. The tester usually has a more powerful antenna

D. The testing tool's NIC is more secure

EXPLANATION

A more powerful antenna could mean the difference between assessing the wireless network for an entire building from your desk versus walking around to each floor with your laptop.

QUESTION 134

With what term from the following list can PING be compared?

A. Pipe

B. Satellite

C. Radio

D. Sonar

EXPLANATION

A signal, called an echo request, is sent out to another computer. The other computer then rebroadcasts the signal, in the form of an echo reply, to the sender.

QUESTION 135

What is the correct statement from the following list?

A. PING can only be used with IP addresses

B. PING can only be used with hostnames

C. PING can be used with hostnames

D. None of the above

EXPLANATION

To determine whether the www.loc.gov site is responding, you could type **ping www.loc.gov** and press Enter. Alternately, you could type **ping 140.147.249.7** (the IP address of this site at the time this book was written) and press Enter.

QUESTION 136

When will you get a "request time out" message as a response to a PING command?

A. Only when a hostname was not found

B. For other reasons besides that the site is not working properly

C. Only when the site is not working properly

D. When multiple sites are found

EXPLANATION

You could also get a "request timed out" message if your workstation is not properly connected to the network, or if the network is malfunctioning.

QUESTION 137

How can you verify that your TCP/IP settings are running?

A. ping 127.0.0.1

B. ping 255.255.0.1

C. ping 127.255.0.0

D. ping 127.127.0.1

EXPLANATION

By pinging the loopback address, you can determine whether your workstation's TCP/IP services are running.

QUESTION 138

Assuming that 200.34.1.15 belongs to a host on a different subnet, how can you verify connectivity with that other subnet?

    A. ping 200.34.1.0

    B. ping 255.34.1.0

    C. ping 200.34.1.15

    D. ping 200.34.255.15

EXPLANATION

By pinging a host on another subnet, you can determine whether the problem lies with a connectivity device between the two subnets.

QUESTION 139

What is a correct ping command?

    A. ping 140.147.249.7 –a

    B. ping –a 140.147.249.7

    C. ping –a 140:147:249:7

    D. ping 140 147 249 7 a

EXPLANATION

A ping command always begins with the word "ping" followed by a hyphen (-) and a switch, followed by a variable pertaining to that switch.

QUESTION 140

What ping switch allows you to specify a number of echo requests to send?

    A. a

    B. e

    C. r

    D. n

EXPLANATION

For example, if you wanted to ping the Library of Congress site with only two echo requests (rather than the standard four that a Windows operating system uses), you could type the command **ping –n 2 www.loc.gov**.

5

QUESTION 141

What can cause a physical connectivity problem?

A. A wrong router configuration

B. An incorrect NIC installation

C. Using a firewall

D. Enabling proxy services

EXPLANATION

A loose NIC will cause connectivity problems.

QUESTION 142

When troubleshooting an older expansion board NIC, what should you use to configure the card? (Choose 2)

A. Firmware

B. LED

C. Jumper

D. DIP switches

EXPLANATION

On older expansion board NICs, rather than using firmware utilities to modify settings, you may need to set a jumper or DIP switch.

QUESTION 143

What is the name for a small, removable piece of plastic that contains a metal receptacle?

A. Jumper

B. DIP switch

C. LED

D. Jump

EXPLANATION

A jumper's metal receptacle fits over a pair of pins on a circuit board to complete a circuit between those two pins.

QUESTION 144

What is the name for a small plastic toggle switch that can represent an "on" or "off" status that indicates a parameter setting?

    A. Jumper

    B. Connector

    C. LED

    D. DIP switch

EXPLANATION

A DIP switch is used to select a parameter value between two possible values.

QUESTION 145

What is the name for the software that enables an attached device to communicate with the computer's operating system?

    A. NOS

    B. Firewall

    C. Device driver

    D. TCP/IP settings

EXPLANATION

When you purchase a computer that already contains an attached peripheral (such as a sound card), the device drivers should already be installed. However, when you add hardware, you must install the device drivers.

QUESTION 146

What is the default interface name for the first NIC detected by a UNIX or Linux operating system?

    A. eth

    B. eth0

    C. eth1

    D. eth2

EXPLANATION

If a second NIC is present, it will be called eth1.

QUESTION 147

What is eth0 called in UNIX and Linux terminology?

A. Interface

B. NIC

C. Ethernet controller

D. Router connection

EXPLANATION

In UNIX and Linux, eth0 and eth1 provide the network interface.

QUESTION 148

How can you know if your NIC is communicating with the network?

A. Checking its temperature

B. Checking its RJ-45 connector

C. Checking its RJ-11 connector

D. Checking its LEDs

EXPLANATION

You can learn about your NIC's functionality simply by looking at it. Most modern NICs have LEDs that indicate whether or not it is working.

QUESTION 149

What LED shows that a NIC is experiencing either incoming or outgoing traffic?

A. TX

B. ACT

C. LNK

D. RX

EXPLANATION

If ACT is blinking, this LED indicates that the NIC is either transmitting or receiving data (in other words, experiencing activity) on the network.

QUESTION 150

How can you know if a NIC is experiencing a lot of traffic?

- **A.** Checking for a lit ACT
- **B.** Checking for a blinking LNK
- **C.** Checking for a blinking ACT
- **D.** Checking for a lit TX

EXPLANATION

If steady (not blinking), ACT indicates that the NIC is experiencing heavy traffic volume.

QUESTION 151

What LED indicates whether or not a NIC is connected to a network?

- **A.** TX
- **B.** ACT
- **C.** LNK
- **D.** RX

EXPLANATION

Basically, a LNK LED shows that a NIC has detected a network. Nothing can be said about traffic activity.

QUESTION 152

What does a blinking LNK mean on some NICs?

- **A.** NIC is not functional
- **B.** No cabling detected
- **C.** No network detected
- **D.** Lack of communication

EXPLANATION

In some models, if a LNK LED is blinking, it means the NIC detects the network but cannot communicate with it.

QUESTION 153

What LED shows outgoing traffic?

  A. TX
  B. LNK
  C. ACT
  D. RX

EXPLANATION

If blinking, TX LED indicates that the NIC is functional and transmitting frames to the network.

QUESTION 154

What LED shows incoming traffic?

  A. TX
  B. RX
  C. ACT
  D. LNK

EXPLANATION

If blinking, RX LED indicates that the NIC is functional and receiving frames from the network.

QUESTION 155

What configuration variable should you consider when troubleshooting a NIC?

  A. Voltage range
  B. LNK value
  C. IRQ
  D. TX/RX values

EXPLANATION

When a device attached to a computer's bus, such as an NIC, requires attention from the computer's processor, it issues an interrupt request.

QUESTION 156

What is the name for a message to the computer that instructs it to stop what it is doing and pay attention to something else?

    A. Interrupt request

    B. Context switch

    C. Plug-and-play

    D. Multiprocessing

EXPLANATION

When a device attached to a computer's bus, such as a keyboard or floppy disk drive, requires attention from the computer's processor, it issues an interrupt request.

QUESTION 157

What is the name of a number that uniquely identifies that component to the main bus?

    A. Jumper number

    B. Interrupt

    C. DPI number

    D. IRQ number

EXPLANATION

An IRQ number is the means by which the bus understands which device to acknowledge.

QUESTION 158

How many IRQ numbers exist on a computer?

    A. 6

    B. 12

    C. 16

    D. 24

EXPLANATION

IRQ numbers range from 0 to 15.

5

QUESTION 159

What is a typical IRQ number used by an NIC?

A. 1
B. 5
C. 9
D. 16

EXPLANATION

On every type of computer, a floppy disk controller claims IRQ 6, and a keyboard controller takes IRQ 1.

QUESTION 160

What will happen if a NIC is trying to use an already assigned IRQ number?

A. The ACT LED will turn red
B. The computer may lock up or "hang" either upon starting or when the operating system is loading
C. The TX LED will blink
D. Nothing

EXPLANATION

If two devices attempt to use the same interrupt, resource conflicts and performance problems will result.

QUESTION 161

How can you solve an IRQ conflict?

A. Reinstall your NOS
B. Restart your computer
C. Reassign a device's IRQ
D. Unplug your keyboard

EXPLANATION

You can view and change IRQ assignments through the operating system.

QUESTION 162

What is the name for the simple set of instructions that enables a computer to initially recognize its hardware?

    A. BIOS
    B. CMOS
    C. IRQ
    D. PCI

EXPLANATION

Once a computer is up and running, the BIOS provides an interface between the computer's software and hardware, allowing it to recognize which device is associated with each IRQ.

5

QUESTION 163

What NIC configuration variable indicates, in hexadecimal notation, the area of memory that the NIC and CPU will use for exchanging, or buffering, data?

    A. IRQ number
    B. Firmware settings
    C. Base I/O port
    D. Memory range

EXPLANATION

As with IRQs, some memory ranges are reserved for specific devices—most notably, the motherboard. Reserved address ranges should never be selected for new devices.

QUESTION 164

What memory area is usually assigned to an NIC?

    A. Low memory area
    B. Middle memory area
    C. High memory area
    D. NICs are not assigned memory ranges

EXPLANATION

NICs typically use a memory range in the A0000–FFFFF range.

QUESTION 165

What is true about memory range conflicts?

    A. They are more common than IRQ conflicts

    B. You may never run into a memory range conflict

    C. They never occur

    D. They are equally common as IRQ conflicts

EXPLANATION

Memory range settings are less likely to cause resource conflicts than IRQ settings, mainly because there are more available memory ranges than IRQs.

QUESTION 166

What NIC configuration variable specifies, in hexadecimal notation, which area of memory will act as a channel for moving data between the NIC and the CPU?

    A. Base I/O port

    B. IRQ number

    C. Firmware settings

    D. Memory range

EXPLANATION

Most NICs use two memory ranges for this channel, and the base I/O port settings identify the beginning of each range.

QUESTION 167

What is true about base I/O ports?

    A. They cannot cause conflicts

    B. They can cause conflicts

    C. NIC's base I/O ports cannot be changed

    D. None of the above

EXPLANATION

Like its IRQ, a device's base I/O port cannot be used by any other device.

QUESTION 168

What NIC configuration variable specifies its transmission characteristics?

   A. Base I/O port

   B. IRQ number

   C. Firmware

   D. Memory range

EXPLANATION

Once you have adjusted the NIC's system resources, you may need to modify its transmission characteristics. These settings are held in the adapter's firmware.

QUESTION 169

5

What are the components of an NIC's firmware?

   A. Configuration data only

   B. A ROM chip only

   C. PROM chip and the data it holds

   D. EEPROM chip and the data it holds

EXPLANATION

When you change the firmware, you are actually writing to the EEPROM chip on the NIC.

QUESTION 170

What is the name for a connector that plugs into a port and crosses over the transmit line to the receive line so that outgoing signals can be redirected into the computer for testing?

   A. Terminal

   B. Loopback plug

   C. Transceiver

   D. Crossover adapter

EXPLANATION

One connectivity test, called a loopback test, requires you to install a loopback plug into the NIC's media connector.

QUESTION 171

On what network topology can a repeater be used?

A. Mesh

B. Ring

C. Star

D. None of the above

EXPLANATION

Repeaters are suited only to bus topology networks.

QUESTION 172

What is the name for a logically or physically distinct Ethernet network segment on which all participating devices must detect and accommodate data collisions?

A. Uplink

B. MAU

C. Collision domain

D. Network domain

EXPLANATION

All devices connected to a hub share the same amount of bandwidth and the same collision domain.

QUESTION 173

What happens if you add nodes to a collision domain?

A. More collisions may appear

B. The network performance is improved

C. The network bandwidth is increased

D. Nothing

EXPLANATION

Suffice it to say that the more nodes participating in the same collision domain, the higher the likelihood of transmission errors and slower performance.

QUESTION 174

What is the name for a device or connection on a network that, were it to fail, could cause the entire network or portion of the network to stop functioning?

  A. Standalone hub
  B. Smart hub
  C. Repeater
  D. Single point of failure

EXPLANATION

The disadvantage to using a single hub for many connections is that you introduce a single point of failure on the network.

QUESTION 175

What type of hub should you use when planning to have a high number of connections?

  A. Standalone
  B. Stackable
  C. Hubby
  D. Hublet

EXPLANATION

Stackable hubs linked together logically represent one large hub to the network. One benefit to using stackable hubs is that your network or workgroup does not depend on a single hub, which could present a single point of failure

QUESTION 176

What connectivity device can extend an Ethernet network without further extending a collision domain, or segment?

  A. Hub
  B. Repeater
  C. Bridge
  D. Router

EXPLANATION

By inserting a bridge into a network, you can add length beyond the maximum limits that apply to segments.

QUESTION 177

What kind of bridge is used to connect the wireless and wire-bound parts of a network?

    A. Smart bridge

    B. Access point

    C. Stackable bridge

    D. Intelligent bridge

EXPLANATION

An access point without bridging functions could only connect an ad-hoc group of wireless clients with each other.

QUESTION 178

What kind of connectivity device can be used to separate each single host on your network into its own collision domain?

    A. Switch

    B. Hub

    C. Repeater

    D. NIC

EXPLANATION

Each port on the switch acts like a bridge, and each device connected to a switch effectively receives its own dedicated channel.

QUESTION 179

What kind of connectivity device can be used to ease traffic congestion in LAN workgroups?

    A. Stackable hub

    B. Repeater

    C. Hublet

    D. Switch

EXPLANATION

Because a switch limits the number of devices in a collision domain, it limits the potential for collisions.

QUESTION 180

What connectivity device is appropriate for applications that transfer a large amount of traffic and are sensitive to time delays?

A. NIC
B. Switch
C. Router
D. Access point

EXPLANATION

Because switches provide separate channels for (potentially) every device, performance stands to gain.

QUESTION 181

5

What is one disadvantage of a switch that may eventually bring your network to a halt?

A. Data loss
B. Security
C. Performance
D. Increased number of collision domains

EXPLANATION

For packets using connectionless protocols, the number of collisions will mount, and eventually all network traffic will grind to a halt.

QUESTION 182

What kind of data flaws can a cut-through switch detect?

A. Corrupt packets
B. Giant
C. Runt
D. Jabber

EXPLANATION

Upon detecting a runt, the switch will wait to transmit that packet until it determines its integrity.

QUESTION 183

When are cut-through switches recommended?

    A. When connecting a small workgroup where speed is not important

    B. When connecting a large workgroup where speed is important

    C. When connecting a large workgroup

    D. When connecting a small workgroup where speed is important

EXPLANATION

The most significant advantage of the cut-through mode is its speed. The time-saving advantages to cut-through switching become insignificant, however, if the switch is flooded with traffic.

QUESTION 184

When are store and forward switches appropriate?

    A. When connecting small networks where speed is important

    B. When connecting large networks where data integrity is important

    C. When connecting large networks where speed is important

    D. When connecting small networks where data integrity is not important

EXPLANATION

Store and forward mode switches are more appropriate for larger LAN environments because they do not propagate data errors.

QUESTION 185

What can you do to allow visitors access to minimal network functions—for example, an Internet connection—without allowing the possibility of access to the company's data stored on servers?

    A. Use a switch to create a VLAN

    B. Use a router to create a VLAN

    C. Use a smarthub to create a VLAN

    D. Use repeaters instead of switches

EXPLANATION

Reasons for using VLANs include separating groups of users who need special security or network functions.

QUESTION 186

What can be a disadvantage in creating VLANs?

A. You can include nodes on groups

B. You can exclude nodes from groups

C. Nodes on a VLAN can listen to traffic from other VLANs

D. Nodes on a VLAN cannot listen to traffic from other VLANs

EXPLANATION

One potential problem in creating VLANs is that by grouping together certain nodes, you can potentially cut off a group from the rest of the network.

QUESTION 187

5

What is an important aspect to consider when troubleshooting a VLAN?

A. That devices are using the right drivers

B. That the appropriate router is used to create it

C. VLAN configuration

D. None of the above

EXPLANATION

You should ensure that all users and devices that need to exchange data can do so after the VLAN is in operation.

QUESTION 188

You are asked to connect a small LAN using switches. What kind of switch will you use for this purpose?

A. Layer 2 switch

B. Layer 3 switch

C. Layer 4 switch

D. Layer 5 switch

EXPLANATION

Higher-layer switches would not be appropriate for use on a small, contained LAN or to connect a group of end users to the network.

QUESTION 189

When are simple routers best suited?
- **A.** As part of your backbone
- **B.** For the Internet
- **C.** When implementing a WAN
- **D.** When implementing a home network

EXPLANATION

Simple, inexpensive routers are often used in small office and home networks and are called SOHO (small office-home office) routers.

QUESTION 190

What is true about SOHO routers?
- **A.** They always have to be heavily configured before they can be used
- **B.** They are complex to install
- **C.** They are easy to install
- **D.** None of the above

EXPLANATION

As with the simple switches described in the previous section, SOHO routers can be added to a network and function properly without significant configuration.

QUESTION 191

What problems may be present in a network that uses static routing?
- **A.** Router's tables are always changing to reflect network changes
- **B.** Router's tables may be invalid after a change in the network structure
- **C.** Static routing is more insecure
- **D.** They accept unroutable packets

EXPLANATION

Static routing is a technique in which a network administrator programs a router to use specific paths between nodes.

QUESTION 192

What problems may be present in a network that uses dynamic routing?
- **A.** It is not commonly used by other networks
- **B.** They do not account for changes in the network
- **C.** The tables contain fixed paths
- **D.** In very unstable environments, router's tables can never reach a stable state

EXPLANATION

If congestion or failures affect the network, a router using dynamic routing can detect the problems and reroute data through a different path.

QUESTION 193

5

What kind of problem can be caused by a gateway?
- **A.** They cannot coexist with switches
- **B.** They cannot coexist with routers
- **C.** Network congestion
- **D.** They require a hub to connect to the network

EXPLANATION

They transmit data more slowly than bridges or routers.

QUESTION 194

What kind of gateway can you use to allow dissimilar networks to communicate with each other?
- **A.** LAN gateway
- **B.** IBM gateway
- **C.** Internet gateway
- **D.** E-mail gateway

EXPLANATION

A LAN gateway allows segments of a LAN running different protocols or different network models to communicate with each other.

QUESTION 195

What kind of gateway can be used to connect a data network with a voice network?

A. Application gateway

B. Internet gateway

C. Phone gateway

D. Voice/data gateway

EXPLANATION

A voice/data gateway connects the part of a network that handles data traffic with the part of a network that handles voice traffic.

QUESTION 196

What is true about transmission flaws?

A. They only affect digital signals

B. They affect analog and digital signals

C. They only affect analog signals

D. They never affect digital signals

EXPLANATION

Both analog and digital signals are susceptible to degradation between the time they are issued by a transmitter and the time they are received.

QUESTION 197

What is a source of EMI?

A. A waterfall

B. A hot surface

C. Televisions

D. None of the above

EXPLANATION

A common source of noise is electromagnetic interference (EMI), or waves that emanate from electrical devices or cables carrying electricity.

QUESTION 198

Radiofrequency interference is a type of

A. EMI

B. Attenuation flaw

C. Latency

D. Signal repeater

EXPLANATION

Radiofrequency interference (RFI) is electromagnetic interference caused by radiowaves.

QUESTION 199

What kind of transmission flaw takes place when you are on the phone and hear the conversation on your second line in the background?

A. Attenuation

B. Latency

C. Reflection

D. Crosstalk

EXPLANATION

Crosstalk occurs when a signal traveling on one wire or cable infringes on the signal traveling over an adjacent wire or cable.

QUESTION 200

What is true about noise?

A. It cannot be controlled

B. A certain amount of noise is unavoidable

C. It can be avoided

D. It can be completely eliminated

EXPLANATION

Engineers have designed a number of ways to limit the potential for noise to degrade a signal.

5

QUESTION 201

What can you do to compensate for signal attenuation?

A. Make your signals stronger

B. Make your signals weaker

C. Use amplifiers with digital signals

D. Use repeaters with analog signals

EXPLANATION

To compensate for attenuation, both analog and digital signals are strengthened en route so they can travel farther.

QUESTION 202

What is true about latency?

A. Switches do not increase latency

B. Latency is not affected by connectivity devices

C. Routers increase latency

D. Hubs increase latency far more that modems

EXPLANATION

The length of the cable involved affects latency, as does the existence of any intervening connectivity device.

QUESTION 203

What is the term for the length of time it takes for a packet to go from sender to receiver, then back from receiver to sender?

A. LTT

B. RTT

C. ATX

D. IPDelay

EXPLANATION

The most common way to measure latency on data networks is by calculating a packet's round trip time (RTT).

QUESTION 204

When does latency cause problems?
- **A.** When combined with attenuation
- **B.** When combined with noise
- **C.** When a transmitting node is expecting data
- **D.** When a receiving node is expecting data

EXPLANATION

If a receiving node does not receive the rest of the data stream within a given time period, it assumes that no more data is coming.

QUESTION 205

5

What should you do to constrain latency on your network?
- **A.** Make your segments bigger
- **B.** Increment the number of segments in your network
- **C.** Comply with your cabling specifications
- **D.** None of the above

EXPLANATION

To constrain the latency and avoid its associated errors, each type of cabling is rated for a maximum number of connected network segments, and each transmission method is assigned a maximum segment length.

QUESTION 206

What kind of cabling has better noise immunity?
- **A.** STP
- **B.** CAT 3
- **C.** CAT 4
- **D.** CAT 5

EXPLANATION

Because of its shielding, STP is more noise resistant than UTP.

QUESTION 207

When troubleshooting a 100BASE-T network that uses CAT 5 cabling, you detect that its segments are at least 400 feet long. What should you recommend?

A. Segments size are OK, so you should look for other potential reasons

B. Segments should be at most 150m long

C. Segments should be at least 1000 feet long

D. Segments should be at most 100m long

EXPLANATION

The maximum segment length for both STP and UTP is 100m, or 328 feet, on 10BASE-T and 100BASE-T networks.

QUESTION 208

When troubleshooting a 10BASE-T network, you realize that one segment comprises 2000 nodes. What can you recommend?

A. Change the router

B. Reduce the number of nodes

C. Add a new hub

D. Increment the number of nodes

EXPLANATION

A 10BASE-T can accommodate a maximum of 1024 nodes.

QUESTION 209

You were asked to analyze a problematic 10BASE-T network. Your analysis shows that between any two nodes the network contain six segments connected by three repeating devices. What rule is this network disobeying?

A. 3-4-5

B. 4-5-3

C. 5-4-3

D. 6-3-3

EXPLANATION

Between two communicating nodes on a 10BASE-T network, the network cannot contain more than five network segments connected by four repeating devices, and no more than three of the segments may be populated.

QUESTION 210

You are asked to change a 10BASE-T network for a Fast Ethernet network. You decide to keep your perfectly working 5-4-3 configuration with your new network. Suddenly after the change, your new Fast Ethernet network does not work properly. What can be the problem?

    A. There are too many repeating devices

    B. Segments are too long

    C. You forgot to change to CAT 2 cabling

    D. 100BASE-T does not support star topology

EXPLANATION

100BASE-T buses can support a maximum of three network segments connected with two repeating devices.

5

QUESTION 211

What of the following network configurations can cause problems?

    A. A 10BASE-T network with two segments and one repeating device

    B. A 100BASE-TX network using CAT 3 cabling

    C. A 90m long 100BASE-T segment

    D. A 90m long 10BASE-T segment

EXPLANATION

100BASE-TX requires CAT 5 or higher unshielded twisted-pair cabling.

QUESTION 212

What can cause a physical connectivity problem on your network?

    A. Using an already assigned IP address

    B. Routing table loss

    C. A poorly configured switch

    D. A badly crimped RJ-45 connector

EXPLANATION

If you don't crimp twisted-pair wires in the correct position in an RJ-45 connector, the cable will fail to transmit or receive data.

QUESTION 213

An organization that is having physical connectivity problems with its network hires you to fix them. You ask for a detailed report of the network structured cable specifications. They present you with the list that follows. What can be causing those problems?

    A. Twisted-pair cables have been twisted less than one-half inch before inserting them into the punch-down block

    B. Bend radius is equal to or greater than four times the diameter of the cable

    C. Cables have 1 inch and a half of exposure before a twisted-pair termination

    D. None of the above

EXPLANATION

To prevent Physical layer failures, do not leave more than 1 inch of exposed (stripped) cable before a twisted-pair termination.

QUESTION 214

When inspecting a 100BASE-T network, you detect that at some points cables are 50 centimeters from fluorescent lamps. What can you say about this?

    A. It may cause Physical layer failures

    B. UTP is resilient to interference

    C. EMI only affects analog signal

    D. This is the recommended distance

EXPLANATION

To prevent Physical layer failures, install cable at least 3 feet away from sources of EMI.

QUESTION 215

What is the command to view full IP configuration information on a Windows XP workstation?

    A. ifconfig –a

    B. ipconfig /all

    C. ifconfig /all

    D. ifconfig –all

EXPLANATION

The command used to view IP information on a Windows XP workstation is ipconfig.

QUESTION 216

What is the command to view full IP configuration information on a Linux workstation?

    A. ipconfig –a

    B. ipconfig /all

    C. ifconfig –a

    D. ipconfig –all

EXPLANATION

To view and edit IP information on a computer running a version of the UNIX or Linux operating system, use the ifconfig command.

QUESTION 217

What utility can be used to terminate TCP/IP settings on a Windows XP workstation?

    A. ping

    B. arp

    C. ifconfig

    D. ipconfig

EXPLANATION

At the command prompt of a Windows XP workstation, type **ipconfig /release** and then press Enter. Your TCP/IP configuration values will be cleared, and both the IP address and subnet mask will revert to 0.0.0.0.

QUESTION 218

What utility will tell you if a Windows XP host is using APIPA?

    A. netstat

    B. ifconfig

    C. ipconfig

    D. winipcfg

EXPLANATION

At the command prompt of a Windows XP workstation, type **ipconfig /all** and then press Enter. If the Autoconfiguration Enabled option is set to Yes, your computer is using APIPA.

QUESTION 219

One morning you detect that each time you try to visit a Web site using your browser, it will show a message similar to "Cannot resolve hostname." What can be the problem?

A. You are unable to contact your DNS server

B. You are unable to contact a router

C. You are unable to contact a switch

D. You are unable to contact your organization's Web server

EXPLANATION

Name servers (or DNS servers) are servers that contain databases of associated names and IP addresses and provide this information to resolvers on request.

QUESTION 220

How can you perform a loopback test for your TCP/IP settings?

A. ipconfig 127.0.0.1

B. ping 127.0.0.1

C. ifconfig 127.0.0.1

D. ipconfig –all

EXPLANATION

By pinging the loopback address, 127.0.0.1, you can determine whether your workstation's TCP/IP services are running.

QUESTION 221

One day you realize that your NetBIOS names and TCP/IP names are the same, so you decide to remove your WINS server, leaving the name resolution to your DNS. Immediately after that your NetBIOS names stop working. Why is that?

A. Your DNS is down

B. WINS servers resolve TCP/IP names

C. DNS servers resolve TCP/IP names

D. DNS servers resolve NetBIOS names only

EXPLANATION

A computer's NetBIOS name and its TCP/IP hostname are different entities, though you can choose to use the same name for the NetBIOS name as you use for the TCP/IP name.

QUESTION 222

After careful thinking, you decide to implement a DHCP server for your network so all your host (servers and workstations) can use dynamic IP addresses. You did it overnight. Next morning, all your NetBIOS names cannot be resolved. What can be the cause of this problem?

- **A.** Your WINS server is down
- **B.** Clients do not know how to contact the WINS server
- **C.** You need to install a DNS when using dynamic IP addresses
- **D.** You need to reconfigure your routing tables

EXPLANATION

WINS servers cannot use a dynamic IP address (such as one assigned by a DHCP server).

QUESTION 223

You are the administrator of a large network. One morning you receive several reports that one specific server cannot be contacted. You go and check its network properties and even though its only protocol suite, NetBEUI, is properly installed and configured, some users cannot contact the server. What can be the problem?

- **A.** Lack of a routable protocol
- **B.** Faulty NIC
- **C.** Power failure
- **D.** Lack of data backup

EXPLANATION

Because NetBEUI lacks a Network layer, it is not routable and therefore is unsuitable for large networks.

QUESTION 224

What utility tool can you use to find the date and time of an IP address lease on a Windows XP host?

- **A.** ping
- **B.** ipconfing
- **C.** ifconfig
- **D.** winipcfg

EXPLANATION

On a command prompt, type **ipconfig /all** and press Enter. If you are connected to a network that uses DHCP, notice the date and time when your lease was obtained and when it is due to expire.

QUESTION 225

Where can you change your IP address on a Windows XP workstation?

    A. In the My Computer properties window

    B. In the main hard disk property window

    C. In the My Network Places properties window

    D. In the Internet Protocol (TCP/IP) properties window

EXPLANATION

If you want to modify your IP address settings, click Use the Following IP Address in the Internet Protocol properties dialog box.

QUESTION 226

What is typically the first thing network professionals do when troubleshooting a TCP/IP connection problem?

    A. Check network cabling

    B. Check routing tables

    C. Issue a ping command to check if TCP/IP is running

    D. None of the above

EXPLANATION

A ping test is typically the first thing network professionals try when troubleshooting a TCP/IP connection problem.

QUESTION 227

What other information can be learned from a ping test besides knowing whether or not your TCP/IP is running?

    A. Default gateway's IP address

    B. Number of packets lost

    C. Subnet mask

    D. WINS server name

EXPLANATION

A ping response also shows the number of packets sent and received and the number of packets lost, if any.

QUESTION 228

Your network implements a bus topology. An analysis detects that it is suffering from signal bouncing. What should you do?

  A. Replace network terminators
  B. Change cabling
  C. Reset your hub
  D. Reset your switch

EXPLANATION

Terminators stop signals after they have reached the end of the wire.

QUESTION 229

This is your first day as the administrator of a bus-based network. You are told that the network is highly affected by static electricity. What should you do?

  A. Turn off your fluorescent lamp
  B. Turn off your cell phone
  C. Disable access points
  D. Check if network is grounded

EXPLANATION

A bus network must be grounded at one end to help remove static electricity that could adversely affect the signal.

QUESTION 230

What is one reason for bad performance on a bus-based network?

  A. Network is using 50-ohm terminators
  B. A slow link with your ISP
  C. Too many nodes
  D. None of the above

EXPLANATION

Although networks based on a bus topology are relatively inexpensive to set up, they do not scale well. As you add more nodes, the network's performance degrades.

QUESTION 231

Why can a bus network be hard to troubleshoot?

A. Because it does not scale well

B. Errors may occur at any intermediate point on a bus network

C. Because it uses CAT 3 cabling

D. Because it cannot support more than 12 nodes

EXPLANATION

Bus networks are difficult to troubleshoot because it is a challenge to identify fault locations.

QUESTION 232

You are the administrator of a network using a simple ring topology. One night you were installing some NOS updates. The next day, one workstation did not want to work properly. Suddenly your whole network could not connect. Can you explain why?

A. NOS updates can cause damage to your hubs

B. After any NOS update, you need to reset your router

C. The workstation could not update its antivirus program

D. Ring topology is an active topology

EXPLANATION

The drawback of a simple ring topology is that a single malfunctioning workstation can disable the network.

QUESTION 233

How can you increase network availability on a ring-based network?

A. Implement a second ring running in the opposite direction as the main ring

B. Implement two rings running in the same direction

C. Use CAT 1 cabling

D. Use fiber-optic repeaters

EXPLANATION

An additional ring running inverse to the main ring acts as a backup path so a single malfunction will not disable the network.

QUESTION 234

What topology will you choose from the following list if you favor fault tolerance?

A. Bus

B. Ring

C. Star

D. Bus–ring

EXPLANATION

On a star topology, each node is separately connected to a central connectivity device.

QUESTION 235

You are hired by a company to design a network implementing a star topology. As part of your job you must mention pros and cons of a star topology. What is a con you should mention?

A. Star topology does not scale well

B. Each LAN segment presents a single point of failure

C. Star topology is not fault tolerant

D. Star topology can only be implemented using fiber-optic cabling

EXPLANATION

A failure in the central connectivity device can take down a LAN segment.

QUESTION 236

What topology will you choose if you are interested in scalability?

A. Ring

B. Bus

C. Star

D. Dual mode ring

EXPLANATION

Because they include a centralized connection point, star topologies can easily be moved, isolated, or interconnected with other networks; they are therefore scalable.

QUESTION 237

What topology are you most likely to encounter when troubleshooting a LAN?

A. Bus
B. Mesh
C. Ring
D. Star

EXPLANATION

Because of their scalability and fault tolerance, the star topology has become the most popular fundamental layout used in contemporary LANs.

QUESTION 238

You are asked to troubleshoot a performance problem on a college campus star-based network with 3,000 users, hundred of network printers, and scores of other devices. You have learned from the network administrator that each segment connects at least 1,000 users. What recommendation can you give to the network administrator?

A. Switch to fiber-optic cabling
B. Reduce the number of users per segment
C. Switch to CAT 3 cabling
D. Change the network to use a ring topology

EXPLANATION

The administrator should use switches to subdivide clients and peripherals into many separate broadcast domains.

QUESTION 239

What are the benefits of a star-wired ring topology? (Choose 2)

A. Reliability
B. Scalability
C. Fault tolerance
D. Faster data transmission

EXPLANATION

The star-wired ring topology uses the physical layout of a star in conjunction with the ring topology's data transmission method.

QUESTION 240

What hybrid topology forms the basis for modern Ethernet and Fast Ethernet networks?

A. Star-wired ring

B. Ring

C. Star-wired bus

D. Bus

EXPLANATION

In a star-wired bus topology, groups of workstations are star-connected to hubs and then networked via a single bus.

QUESTION 241

5

Suppose you manage a small star-wired bus topology network in which a single hub serves a workgroup of eight users. How can you add more users at the minimum cost?

A. Changing your routers

B. Buying a new state-of-the-art switch

C. Switching to fiber-optic cabling

D. Using a serial backbone

EXPLANATION

When new employees are added to that department and you need more network connections, you could connect a second hub to the first hub in a daisy chain fashion.

QUESTION 242

How many hubs can you connect on a serial backbone of a 100BASE-TX network before affecting its functionality?

A. 1

B. 2

C. 3

D. 4

EXPLANATION

A 100BASE-TX network can comprise a maximum of three segments connected by two connectivity devices.

QUESTION 243

What kind of backbone will you choose if you want to segregate workgroups and therefore manage them more easily?

A. Distributed backbone

B. Serial backbone

C. Daisy chain backbone

D. None of the above

EXPLANATION

In a star-wired bus topology, groups of workstations are star-connected to hubs and then networked via a single bus.

QUESTION 244

As a good network administrator, you should be able to differentiate between backbone topologies. What kind of backbone has a router or switch as the single central connection point for multiple subnetworks?

A. Daisy chain backbone

B. Distributed backbone

C. Serial backbone

D. Collapsed backbone

EXPLANATION

In a collapsed backbone, a single router or switch is the highest layer of the backbone.

QUESTION 245

You are troubleshooting a network that implements a collapsed backbone. The entire network is down. Individual LANs have connectivity within their domains, but there is no connectivity across LANs. What could be the problem?

A. A power failure in one individual LAN can bring down the entire network

B. One internal switch is down

C. The central router is down

D. One LAN is suffering from traffic congestion

EXPLANATION

In a collapsed backbone topology, a failure in the central router or switch can bring down the entire network.

QUESTION 246

You were hired to help lower costs in the implementation of a parallel backbone. What can you do to help?

    A. Implement parallel connections to only some of the most critical devices on your network

    B. Do not use redundant links

    C. Create duplicate links to ensure reliability

    D. All of the above

EXPLANATION

Although a parallel backbone requires all links to be redundant (duplicated), by selectively implementing the parallel structure, you can lower connectivity costs.

QUESTION 247

What is the next step when logging into a server after the client launches the client software from his desktop?

    A. Powering up his machine

    B. Turning on his NIC

    C. Identifying himself with the server

    D. Calling the redirector

EXPLANATION

When a client tries to log into a server, he first launches the client software from his desktop. Then he enters his credentials (normally, a username and password) and presses the Enter key.

QUESTION 248

What does a redirector do if a request was meant for the client rather than the server?

    A. It sends the request to the server

    B. It decrypts the client's username and password before transmitting it to the server

    C. It encrypts the client's username and password before transmitting it to the server

    D. None of the above

EXPLANATION

If the redirector had determined that the request was meant for the client, rather than the server, it would have issued the request to the client's processor.

QUESTION 249

After entering her name and password, a user receives an error message indicating that the username or password is invalid. What does this problem tell you?

A. Username and password are correct
B. The Physical layer is working
C. The central router is down
D. The network is suffering from traffic congestion

EXPLANATION

You know that at least the physical connection is working because the request reached the NOS, and the NOS attempted to verify the username.

QUESTION 250

What components on the client's side are involved every time a client issues a request for the server?

A. NOS
B. Redirector
C. Client software
D. All of the above

EXPLANATION

For example, if you wished to open a file on the server's hard disk, you would interact with your workstation's operating system to make the file request. The file request would then be intercepted by the redirector and passed to the server via the client software.

QUESTION 251

What is the name for the protocol that enables one system to access resources stored on another system?

A. File access protocol
B. Resource access protocol
C. Shared resources mapping protocol
D. File mapping protocol

EXPLANATION

For example, Windows Server 2003 and Windows XP clients communicate through the Common Internet File System (CIFS) file access protocol.

QUESTION 252

What client software package does Novell recommend to install on Windows XP workstations to connect with a Novell-based server?

- **A.** Client for Microsoft Networks
- **B.** Client for CIFS
- **C.** Client for SMB
- **D.** None of the above

EXPLANATION

Novell recommends installing Novell Client for Windows NT/2000/XP on Windows 2000 or Windows XP workstations.

QUESTION 253

5

What utility can you use on a Linux workstation to obtain the port number where a particular TCP/IP service is running?

- **A.** ping
- **B.** ipconfig
- **C.** netstat
- **D.** winipcfg

EXPLANATION

The netstat utility displays TCP/IP statistics and details about TCP/IP components and connections on a host.

QUESTION 254

Suppose you are a network administrator in charge of maintaining a Web server for an organization. You discover that your Web server, which has multiple processors, sufficient hard disk space, and multiple NICs, is suddenly taking twice as long to respond to HTTP requests. What utility can you use to determine the characteristics of the traffic going into and out of each network interface card?

- **A.** winipcfg
- **B.** netstat
- **C.** arp
- **D.** nbtstat

EXPLANATION

Using netstat, you may discover that one network card is consistently handling 80% of the traffic, even though you had configured the server to share traffic equally among the two.

QUESTION 255

What command allows you to display the routing table on a given machine?

    A. ntbstat -r
    B. arp -r
    C. ipconfig -r
    D. netstat -r

EXPLANATION

The –r switch when used with netstat provides a list of routing table information.

QUESTION 256

What switch should you use to specify to netstat what protocol statistics to list?

    A. -p
    B. -r
    C. -e
    D. -s

EXPLANATION

netstat –p TCP displays statistics about TCP connections.

QUESTION 257

You are troubleshooting a network that runs NetBIOS over TCP/IP. What command can you use to display a machine's name table if you know its NetBIOS name?

    A. netstat –A name
    B. netstat –a name
    C. nbtstat –a name
    D. nbtstat –A name

EXPLANATION

The –a switch when used with nbtstat displays a machine's name table given its NetBIOS name; the name of the machine must be supplied after the -a switch.

QUESTION 258

What nbtstat switch can be used to display statistics about names that have been resolved to IP addresses by broadcast and by WINS?

    A. -p

    B. -r

    C. -w

    D. -A

EXPLANATION

The –r switch is useful for determining whether a workstation is resolving names properly or for determining whether WINS is operating correctly.

QUESTION 259

What nbtstat switch displays a list of all the current NetBIOS sessions for a machine?

    A. -a

    B. -e

    C. -r

    D. -s

EXPLANATION

The nbtstat –s command attempts to resolve IP addresses to NetBIOS names in the listing; if the machine has no current NetBIOS connections, the result of this command will indicate that fact.

QUESTION 260

What is a very useful tool for troubleshooting DNS resolution problems?

    A. nslookup

    B. netstat

    C. arp

    D. nbtstat

EXPLANATION

The nslookup utility allows you to query the DNS database from any computer on the network and find the hostname of a device by specifying its IP address, or vice versa.

QUESTION 261

What utility can be even more useful than nslookup when troubleshooting DNS problems?

- **A.** ipconfig
- **B.** netstat
- **C.** dig
- **D.** nbtstat

EXPLANATION

The dig utility comes with over two dozen switches, making it much more flexible than nslookup.

QUESTION 262

You are the administrator of a small network. One morning you noticed your network received a flood of messages that originated from www.trinketmakers.com, so you decided to contact them. What tool can you use to find out who leases the trinketmakers.com domain?

- **A.** arp
- **B.** whois
- **C.** finger
- **D.** netstat

EXPLANATION

The utility that allows you to query the DNS registration database and obtain information about a domain is called whois.

QUESTION 263

You are the administrator of a large network. Your network is having subnet connectivity problems, so you decide to troubleshoot them. What is a good tool for this purpose?

- **A.** tracert
- **B.** nslookup
- **C.** finger
- **D.** arp

EXPLANATION

The traceroute utility (known as tracert on Windows-based systems) uses ICMP to trace the path from one networked node to another, identifying all intermediate hops between the two nodes.

QUESTION 264

How can you instruct the traceroute command not to resolve IP addresses to hostnames?
  A. Using the −a switch
  B. Using the −p switch
  C. Using the −r switch
  D. Using the −d switch

EXPLANATION

By adding −d to a traceroute command, it will not resolve IP addresses.

QUESTION 265

What traceroute switch specifies the maximum number of hops the packets should take when attempting to reach a host?
  A. -d
  B. -h
  C. -n
  D. -p

EXPLANATION

For example, traceroute −h 12 would indicate a maximum of 12 hops.

QUESTION 266

What switch should you use to change the time traceroute waits for a response?
  A. -o
  B. -t
  C. -w
  D. -d

EXPLANATION

The −w switch identifies a timeout period for responses.

QUESTION 267

How can you view the TCP/IP information associated with every interface on a Linux-based workstation?

    A. ifconfig –a
    B. ipconfig –a
    C. ifconfig /all
    D. winipcfg /all

EXPLANATION

ifconfig –a applies the command to all interfaces on a device.

QUESTION 268

What ifconfig switch allows you to deactivate a network interface on a UNIX-based device?

    A. off
    B. deact
    C. up
    D. down

EXPLANATION

The down switch marks the interface as unavailable to the network.

QUESTION 269

What ifconfig switch allows you to reactivate a network interface on a UNIX-based system?

    A. up
    B. on
    C. act
    D. react

EXPLANATION

The up switch reinitializes the interface after it has been taken "down," so that it is once again available to the network.

QUESTION 270

What utility can you use to renew a DHCP lease on a Windows 95 workstation?
- **A.** ipconfig
- **B.** winipcfg
- **C.** ifconfig
- **D.** nslookup

EXPLANATION

As with the ipconfig utility, you can release or renew DHCP-assigned addresses through the winipcfg dialog box.

QUESTION 271

What is a good tip to be a successful troubleshooter?
- **A.** Be fast
- **B.** Easily jump to conclusions
- **C.** Be organized
- **D.** None of the above

EXPLANATION

Successful troubleshooters proceed logically and methodically.

QUESTION 272

What is a good general rule for troubleshooting?
- **A.** Do not waste your time on obvious things
- **B.** Sometimes the answer is obvious
- **C.** Pay attention only to complex things
- **D.** Do not ask simple questions

EXPLANATION

A good, general rule for troubleshooting can be stated as follows: Pay attention to the obvious!

QUESTION 273

What kind of problem is when a router is not properly connected to the backbone?

A. Application layer problem
B. Network layer problem
C. Logical connectivity problem
D. Physical connectivity problem

EXPLANATION

You can spot a Physical layer problem by answering this question: Is the hub, router, or switch properly connected to the backbone?

QUESTION 274

You were applying some patches to one of your workstations. Next morning that equipment has problems logging into the network. What kind of problem are you facing?

A. Logical connectivity problem
B. Update problem
C. Physical connectivity problem
D. Physical layer problem

EXPLANATION

You can spot a logical connectivity problem by answering the following question: Has an operating system, configuration, or application been recently changed, introduced, or deleted?

QUESTION 275

One day you receive a call from one of your network users. She cannot connect to the network for the last two hours. When you go and check her machine, you notice that the wrong server is selected as the default. What kind of problem is this?

A. Physical connectivity problem
B. Transport layer problem
C. Logical connectivity problem
D. Data Link layer problem

EXPLANATION

You can spot a logical connectivity problem by answering the following question: Has an operating system, configuration, or application been recently changed, introduced, or deleted?

QUESTION 276

One of your print servers is experiencing connectivity problems. After a few minutes you found out that a mouse has chewed through the connecting cable. What kind of problem is this?

    A. Application layer problem

    B. Physical layer problem

    C. Transport layer problem

    D. Network layer problem

EXPLANATION

You can spot a physical connectivity problem by answering the following question: Are all cables in good condition (without signs of wear or damage)?

5

QUESTION 277

You were hired to troubleshoot a medium-size network. After asking a few questions and taking some notes, you find that the network is having a physical connectivity problem. Select from the following list what could have caused this problem:

    A. An RJ-45 connector for your network router is broken

    B. The network administrator has changed his password

    C. You updated the authentication server's NOS

    D. All of the above

EXPLANATION

When looking for physical connectivity problems, verify that all connectors (for example, RJ-45) are in good condition and properly seated.

QUESTION 278

What tool can you use to check for local collisions on Ethernet?

    A. ipconfig

    B. nslookup

    C. Protocol analyzers

    D. Network monitors

EXPLANATION

A network monitor is a software-based tool that continually monitors network traffic from a server or workstation attached to the network.

QUESTION 279

You just purchased a cable labeled "CAT 6." How can you prove that this cable is really a CAT 6 cable?

- **A.** Use a tone generator or tone locator tester
- **B.** Use a multimeter
- **C.** Use a cable performance tester
- **D.** There is no need to prove it since you bought the cable from a reputable vendor

EXPLANATION

Besides testing for cable continuity, a cable performance tester issues pass/fail ratings for CAT 3, CAT 5, CAT 5e, CAT 6, or CAT 7 standards.

QUESTION 280

Somebody asked you to measure the attenuation on a new cable he bought. What is an appropriate tool for this purpose?

- **A.** A cable performance tester
- **B.** A cable continuity tester
- **C.** A multimeter
- **D.** None of the above

EXPLANATION

Besides testing for cable continuity, a cable performance tester can measure attenuation along a cable.

ANSWER GRID FOR CORE DOMAIN 4

Question	Answer	Objective	Question	Answer	Objective
1	A	4.8	11	B	4.8
2	C	4.8	12	D	4.8
3	D	4.8	13	C	4.8
4	B	4.8	14	A	4.8
5	C	4.8	15	B	4.1, 4.2
6	D	4.8	16	A	4.1, 4.2
7	B	4.8	17	A	4.1, 4.2
8	A	4.8	18	C	4.5
9	B	4.8	19	B	4.5
10	C	4.8	20	D	4.5

Question	Answer	Objective
21	C	4.5
22	C	4.1, 4.2
23	A	4.1, 4.2
24	A	4.1, 4.2
25	B	4.1, 4.2
26	C	4.1, 4.2
27	D	4.1, 4.2
28	B	4.1, 4.2
29	A	4.1, 4.2
30	D	4.1, 4.2
31	C	4.1, 4.2
32	B	4.1, 4.2
33	A	4.1, 4.2
34	D	4.1, 4.2
35	B	4.1, 4.2
36	D	4.1, 4.2
37	C	4.1, 4.2
38	B	4.1, 4.2
39	B	4.1, 4.2
40	A	4.1, 4.2
41	C, D	4.1, 4.2
42	D	4.1, 4.2
43	A, B	4.1, 4.2
44	C	4.1, 4.2
45	B, D	4.1, 4.2
46	A	4.1, 4.2
47	C	4.1, 4.2
48	D	4.1, 4.2
49	B	4.1, 4.2
50	A	4.1, 4.2
51	C	4.9
52	B	4.9
53	D	4.9
54	D	4.9
55	A	4.9
56	B	4.9
57	C	4.9
58	D	4.9
59	B	4.9
60	A	4.9

Question	Answer	Objective
61	C	4.9
62	D	4.9
63	A, B	4.9
64	B, C	4.9
65	D	4.9
66	A	4.9
67	B	4.9
68	C, D	4.9
69	A, C	4.9
70	D	4.9
71	A, C	4.8, 4.9
72	D	4.8, 4.9
73	B	4.8, 4.9
74	C	4.8, 4.9
75	A	4.8, 4.9
76	B	4.6, 4.9
77	D	4.6, 4.9
78	B	4.6, 4.9
79	C	4.6, 4.9
80	A	4.8, 4.9
81	B	4.8, 4.9
82	D	4.8, 4.9
83	B	4.8, 4.9
84	C	4.8, 4.9
85	A	4.8, 4.9
86	D	4.9
87	C	4.9
88	B	4.9
89	D	4.9
90	A	4.9
91	B, D	4.9
92	C	4.9
93	A	4.9
94	B	4.9
95	D	4.9
96	C	4.9
97	A	4.9
98	C	4.9
99	B	4.9
100	D	4.9

5

Question	Answer	Objective	Question	Answer	Objective
101	A	4.9	141	B	4.4
102	B	4.9	142	C, D	4.4
103	D	4.9	143	A	4.4
104	C, D	4.9	144	D	4.4
105	A	4.2, 4.8	145	C	4.4
106	B	4.2, 4.8	146	B	4.5
107	C	4.2, 4.8	147	A	4.5
108	D	4.2, 4.8	148	D	4.3
109	A	4.2, 4.8	149	B	4.3
110	C	4.2, 4.8	150	A	4.3
111	B	4.2, 4.8	151	C	4.3
112	D	4.2, 4.8	152	D	4.3
113	A	4.2, 4.8	153	A	4.3
114	C	4.2, 4.8	154	B	4.3
115	B	4.2, 4.8	155	C	4.4, 4.5
116	A	4.2, 4.8	156	A	4.4, 4.5
117	D	4.2, 4.8	157	D	4.4, 4.5
118	C	4.2, 4.8	158	C	4.4, 4.5
119	B	4.2, 4.8	159	C	4.4, 4.5
120	A	4.2, 4.8	160	B	4.4, 4.5
121	D	4.2, 4.8	161	C	4.4, 4.5
122	B	4.2, 4.8	162	A	4.4, 4.5
123	C	4.2, 4.8	163	D	4.4, 4.5
124	A	4.2, 4.8	164	C	4.4, 4.5
125	A	4.2, 4.8	165	B	4.4, 4.5
126	B	4.2, 4.8	166	A	4.4, 4.5
127	D	4.8	167	B	4.4, 4.5
128	C	4.8	168	C	4.4, 4.5
129	D	4.8	169	D	4.4, 4.5
130	A	4.8	170	B	4.4, 4.5
131	B	4.8	171	D	4.7
132	B	4.8	172	C	4.7
133	C	4.8	173	A	4.7
134	D	4.1, 4.2	174	D	4.7
135	C	4.1, 4.2	175	B	4.7
136	B	4.1, 4.2	176	C	4.8
137	A	4.1, 4.2	177	B	4.8
138	C	4.1, 4.2	178	A	4.8
139	B	4.1, 4.2	179	D	4.8
140	D	4.1, 4.2	180	B	4.8

Question	Answer	Objective		Question	Answer	Objective
181	A	4.8		221	C	4.6
182	C	4.8		222	D	4.6
183	D	4.8		223	A	4.6
184	B	4.8		224	B	4.1, 4.2
185	A	4.8		225	D	4.1, 4.2
186	B	4.8		226	C	4.1, 4.2
187	C	4.8		227	B	4.1, 4.2
188	A	4.8		228	A	4.7
189	D	4.4		229	D	4.7
190	C	4.4		230	C	4.7
191	B	4.8		231	B	4.7
192	D	4.8		232	D	4.7
193	C	4.8		233	A	4.7
194	A	4.8		234	C	4.7
195	D	4.8		235	B	4.7
196	B	4.4		236	C	4.7
197	C	4.4		237	D	4.7
198	A	4.4		238	B	4.7
199	D	4.4		239	A, C	4.7
200	B	4.4		240	C	4.7
201	A	4.4		241	D	4.7
202	C	4.4		242	B	4.7
203	B	4.4		243	A	4.7
204	D	4.4		244	D	4.7
205	C	4.4		245	C	4.7
206	A	4.4		246	A	4.7
207	D	4.4		247	C	4.5
208	B	4.4		248	D	4.5
209	C	4.4		249	B	4.5
210	A	4.4		250	D	4.5
211	B	4.7		251	A	4.5
212	D	4.4		252	D	4.5
213	C	4.8		253	C	4.1, 4.2
214	A	4.7		254	B	4.1, 4.2
215	B	4.1, 4.2		255	D	4.1, 4.2
216	C	4.1, 4.2		256	A	4.1, 4.2
217	D	4.1, 4.2		257	C	4.1, 4.2
218	C	4.1, 4.2		258	B	4.1, 4.2
219	A	4.6		259	D	4.1, 4.2
220	B	4.1, 4.2		260	A	4.1, 4.2

5

Question	Answer	Objective	Question	Answer	Objective
261	C	4.1, 4.2	271	C	4.9
262	B	4.1, 4.2	272	B	4.9
263	A	4.1, 4.2	273	D	4.8, 4.9
264	D	4.1, 4.2	274	A	4.6, 4.9
265	B	4.1, 4.2	275	C	4.6, 4.9
266	C	4.1, 4.2	276	B	4.8, 4.9
267	A	4.1, 4.2	277	A	4.9
268	D	4.1, 4.2	278	D	4.2, 4.8
269	A	4.1, 4.2	279	C	4.8
270	B	4.1, 4.2	280	A	4.8

A

NETWORK+ (2005) EXAMINATION OBJECTIVES

DOMAIN 1.0 — MEDIA AND TOPOLOGIES — 20%

1.1 Recognize the following logical or physical network topologies given a diagram, schematic, or description:

- Star
- Bus
- Mesh
- Ring

1.2 Specify the main features of 802.2 (Logical Link Control), 802.3 (Ethernet), 802.5 (Token Ring), 802.11 (wireless), and FDDI (Fiber Distributed Data Interface) networking technologies, including:

- Speed
- Access method (CSMA/CA (Carrier Sense Multiple Access/Collision Avoidance) and CSMA/CD (Carrier Sense Multiple Access/Collision Detection))
- Topology
- Media

1.3 Specify the characteristics (for example: speed, length, topology, and cable type) of the following cable standards:

- 10BASE-T and 10BASE-FL
- 100BASE-TX and 100BASE-FX
- 1000BASE-T, 1000BASE-CX, 1000BASE-SX, and 1000BASE-LX
- 10 GBASE-SR, 10 GBASE-LR, and 10 GBASE-ER

1.4 Recognize the following media connectors and describe their uses:

- RJ-11 (Registered Jack)
- RJ-45 (Registered Jack)
- F-Type
- ST (Straight Tip)
- SC (Subscriber Connector or Standard Connector)
- IEEE 1394 (FireWire)
- Fiber LC (Local Connector)
- MT-RJ (Mechanical Transfer Registered Jack)
- USB (Universal Serial Bus)

1.5 Recognize the following media types and describe their uses:

- Category 3, 5, 5e, and 6
- UTP (Unshielded Twisted Pair)
- STP (Shielded Twisted Pair)
- Coaxial cable
- SMF (Single Mode Fiber) optic cable
- MMF (Multimode Fiber) optic cable

1.6 Identify the purposes, features, and functions of the following network components:

- Hubs
- Switches
- Bridges
- Routers
- Gateways
- CSU/DSU (Channel Service Unit/Data Service Unit)
- NICs (network interface card)
- ISDN (Integrated Services Digital Network) adapters
- WAP (Wireless Access Point)
- Modems
- Transceivers (media converters)
- Firewalls

1.7 Specify the general characteristics (for example: carrier speed, frequency, transmission type, and topology) of the following wireless technologies:

- 802.11 (Frequency hopping spread spectrum)
- 802.11x (Direct sequence spread spectrum)
- Infrared
- Bluetooth

1.8 Identify factors that affect the range and speed of wireless service (for example: interference, antenna type, and environmental factors).

DOMAIN 2.0 — PROTOCOLS AND STANDARDS — 20%

2.1 Identify a MAC (Media Access Control) address and its parts.

2.2 Identify the seven layers of the OSI (Open Systems Interconnect) Model and their functions.

2.3 Identify the OSI (Open Systems Interconnect) layers at which the following network components operate:

- Hubs
- Switches
- Bridges
- Routers
- NICs (network interface card)
- WAPs (Wireless Access Point)

2.4 Differentiate between the following network protocols in terms of routing, addressing schemes, interoperability, and naming conventions:

- IPX/SPX (Internetwork Packet Exchange/Sequence Packet Exchange)
- NetBEUI (Network Basic Input/Output System Extended User Interface)
- AppleTalk/AppleTalk over IP (Internet Protocol)
- TCP/IP (Transmission Control Protocol/Internet Protocol)

2.5 Identify the components and structure of IP (Internet Protocol) addresses (IPv4, IPv6) and the required setting for connections across the Internet.

2.6 Identify classful IP (Internet Protocol) ranges and their subnet masks (for example: Class A, B, and C).

2.7 Identify the purpose of subnetting.

A

2.8 Identify the differences between private and public network addressing schemes.

2.9 Identify and differentiate between the following IP (Internet Protocol) addressing methods:

- Static

- Dynamic

- Self-assigned (APIPA (Automatic Private Internet Protocol Addressing))

2.10 Define the purpose, function and use of the following protocols used in the TCP/IP (Transmission Control Protocol/Internet Protocol) suite:

- TCP (Transmission Control Protocol)

- UDP (User Datagram Protocol)

- FTP (File Transfer Protocol)

- SFTP (Secure File Transfer Protocol)

- TFTP (Trivial File Transfer Protocol)

- SMTP (Simple Mail Transfer Protocol)

- HTTP (Hypertext Transfer Protocol)

- HTTPS (Hypertext Transfer Protocol Secure)

- POP3/IMAP4 (Post Office Protocol version 3/Internet Message Access Protocol version 4)

- Telnet

- SSH (Secure Shell)

- ICMP (Internet Control Message Protocol)

- ARP/RARP (Address Resolution Protocol/Reverse Address Resolution Protocol)

- NTP (Network Time Protocol)

- NNTP (Network News Transport Protocol)

- SCP (Secure Copy Protocol)

- LDAP (Lightweight Directory Access Protocol)

- IGMP (Internet Group Multicast Protocol)

- LPR (Line Printer Remote)

2.11 Define the function of TCP/UDP (Transmission Control Protocol/User Datagram Protocol) ports.

2.12 Identify the well-known ports associated with the following commonly used services and protocols:

- 20 FTP (File Transfer Protocol)
- 21 FTP (File Transfer Protocol)
- 22 SSH (Secure Shell)
- 23 Telnet
- 25 SMTP (Simple Mail Transfer Protocol)
- 53 DNS (Domain Name Service)
- 69 TFTP (Trivial File Transfer Protocol)
- 80 HTTP (Hypertext Transfer Protocol)
- 110 POP3 (Post Office Protocol version 3)
- 119 NNTP (Network News Transport Protocol)
- 123 NTP (Network Time Protocol)
- 143 IMAP4 (Internet Message Access Protocol version 4)
- 443 HTTPS (Hypertext Transfer Protocol Secure)

2.13 Identify the purpose of network services and protocols (for example: DNS (Domain Name Service), NAT (Network Address Translation), ICS (Internet Connection Sharing), WINS (Windows Internet Name Service), SNMP (Simple Network Management Protocol), NFS (Network File System), Zeroconf (Zero configuration), SMB (Server Message Block), AFP (Apple File Protocol), LPD (Line Printer Daemon), and Samba).

2.14 Identify the basic characteristics (for example: speed, capacity, and media) of the following WAN (Wide Area Networks) technologies:

- Packet switching
- Circuit switching
- ISDN (Integrated Services Digital Network)
- FDDI (Fiber Distributed Data Interface)
- T1 (T Carrier level 1)/E1/J1
- T3 (T Carrier level 3)/E3/J3
- OCx (Optical Carrier)
- X.25

A

2.15 Identify the basic characteristics of the following internet access technologies:

- xDSL (Digital Subscriber Line)
- Broadband Cable (Cable modem)
- POTS/PSTN (Plain Old Telephone Service/Public Switched Telephone Network)
- Satellite
- Wireless

2.16 Define the function of the following remote access protocols and services:

- RAS (Remote Access Service)
- PPP (Point-to-Point Protocol)
- SLIP (Serial Line Internet Protocol)
- PPPoE (Point-to-Point Protocol over Ethernet)
- PPTP (Point-to-Point Tunneling Protocol)
- VPN (Virtual Private Network)
- RDP (Remote Desktop Protocol)

2.17 Identify the following security protocols and describe their purpose and function:

- IPSec (Internet Protocol Security)
- L2TP (Layer 2 Tunneling Protocol)
- SSL (Secure Sockets Layer)
- WEP (Wired Equivalent Privacy)
- WPA (Wi-Fi Protected Access)
- 802.1x

2.18 Identify authentication protocols (for example: CHAP (Challenge Handshake Authentication Protocol), MS-CHAP (Microsoft Challenge Handshake Authentication Protocol), PAP (Password Authentication Protocol), RADIUS (Remote Authentication Dial-In User Service), Kerberos, and EAP (Extensible Authentication Protocol)).

DOMAIN 3.0 — NETWORK IMPLEMENTATION — 25%

3.1 Identify the basic capabilities (for example: client support, interoperability, authentication, file and print services, application support, and security) of the following server operating systems to access network resources:

- UNIX/Linux/Mac OS X Server

- Netware

- Windows

- Appleshare IP (Internet Protocol)

3.2 Identify the basic capabilities needed for client workstations to connect to and use network resources (for example: media, network protocols, and peer and server services).

3.3 Identify the appropriate tool for a given wiring task (for example: wire crimper, media tester/certifier, punch down tool, or tone generator).

3.4 Given a remote connectivity scenario comprised of a protocol, an authentication scheme, and physical connectivity, configure the connection. Includes connection to the following servers:

- UNIX/Linux/MAC OS X Server

- Netware

- Windows

- Appleshare IP (Internet Protocol)

3.5 Identify the purpose, benefits, and characteristics of using a firewall.

3.6 Identify the purpose, benefits, and characteristics of using a proxy service.

3.7 Given a connectivity scenario, determine the impact on network functionality of a particular security implementation (for example: port blocking/filtering, authentication, and encryption).

3.8 Identify the main characteristics of VLANs (Virtual Local Area Networks).

3.9 Identify the main characteristics and purpose of extranets and intranets.

3.10 Identify the purpose, benefits and characteristics of using antivirus software.

3.11 Identify the purpose and characteristics of fault tolerance:

- Power

- Link redundancy

- Storage

- Services

A

3.12 Identify the purpose and characteristics of disaster recovery:

- Backup/restore

- Offsite storage

- Hot and cold spares

- Hot, warm, and cold sites

DOMAIN 4.0 — NETWORK SUPPORT — 35%

4.1 Given a troubleshooting scenario, select the appropriate network utility from the following:

- tracert/traceroute

- ping

- arp

- netstat

- nbtstat

- ipconfig/ifconfig

- winipcfg

- nslookup/dig

4.2 Given output from a network diagnostic utility (for example: those utilities listed in objective 4.1), identify the utility and interpret the output.

4.3 Given a network scenario, interpret visual indicators (for example: link LEDs (light emitting diodes) and collision LEDs (light emitting diodes)) to determine the nature of a stated problem.

4.4 Given a troubleshooting scenario involving a client accessing remote network services, identify the cause of the problem (for example: file services, print services, authentication failure, protocol configuration, physical connectivity, and SOHO (Small Office/Home Office) router).

4.5 Given a troubleshooting scenario between a client and the following server environments, identify the cause of a stated problem:

- UNIX/Linux/Mac OS X Server

- Netware

- Windows

- Appleshare IP (Internet Protocol)

4.6 Given a scenario, determine the impact of modifying, adding, or removing network services (for example: DHCP (Dynamic Host Configuration Protocol), DNS (Domain Name Service), and WINS (Windows Internet Name Service)) for network resources and users.

4.7 Given a troubleshooting scenario involving a network with a particular physical topology (for example: bus, star, mesh, or ring) and including a network diagram, identify the network area affected, and the cause of the stated failure.

4.8 Given a network troubleshooting scenario involving an infrastructure (for example: wired or wireless) problem, identify the cause of a stated problem (for example: bad media, interference, network hardware, or environment).

4.9 Given a network problem scenario, select an appropriate course of action based on a logical troubleshooting strategy. This strategy can include the following steps:

1. Identify the symptoms and potential causes
2. Identify the affected area
3. Establish what has changed
4. Select the most probable cause
5. Implement an action plan and solution, including potential effects
6. Test the result
7. Identify the results and effects of the solution
8. Document the solution and process

A

Index

W

Well Known ports, 100
whois, 199–200, 274
wide area networks (WAN)
  designing fault tolerance in, 163
  Dial-back WAN links, 165
Windows 2000, 202
Windows 9x, 203
Windows Active Directory, 130
Windows Me, 203
Windows NT, 202
Windows NT domain data, 130
Windows Server 2003, 124–125, 194, 202, 270
Windows Services for UNIX, 125
Windows XP
  CIFS, and, 194, 270
  ifconfig, and, 203
  IP address changes and, 262
  ipconfig, and, 94–95, 97, 192, 202, 258, 259, 261
  Novell, and, 271
  winipcfg, and, 202
winipcfg, 202, 203, 277
WINS, 111, 260–261, 273
wireless frequency rights, granting exclusive, 30
wireless LAN (WLAN)
  access points, 42–43
  ad hoc, 42
  advantages and disadvantages, 35–36, 44–45

  antennas, 31–32
  attenuation, 35
  fading, 35
  fixed wireless systems, 39
  frequencies, 41
  integrating with wire-bound networks, 44–45
  interference, 37
  line-of-sight (LOS), 33
  maximum distance between access points, 44
  mobile wireless systems, 40, 56
  monitoring, 229
  noise, 35
  obstructions to, 33–34
  problems with, 33–37
  range, 33
  signal types, 29
  standards for, 45
  testing, 230–231
  transmitting through, 31
wireless spectrum, 30
wiring, horizontal, 27
wiring systems, 26. *see also* **cables**
WLAN, 29, 42
workstations, 118
worms, 152

X

X.25, 114